"This is a truly engaging and accessible book, ai
stage in their private practice journey. The lands
siderably in recent years, not least due to the Co
Sarantakis address wide-ranging issues from the
our target market through to working online and the   ....
porary context. As such it is as valuable for trainee tl   ..... those just beginning
to consider setting up in private practice as it is for practitioners such as myself who
have been established for many years. Appropriately for a book about relational ethics it explores the various topics experientially, using thought-provoking case studies
and exercises to prompt the reader to consider their own responses to ethical issues,
rather than providing binary solutions. Solidarity, Compassion and Justice are themes
throughout the book and I felt held by the authors' commitment to those tenets.
A long-overdue book in my view, one I highly recommend to anyone interested in the
ethics of therapeutic work, not just those in private practice."

Susan Utting-Simon, *Senior Accredited Counsellor,*
Psychotherapist & Supervisor in private practice, former Chair of
BACP Private Practice Division

"This book offers a very comprehensive, in-depth and thorough exploration of the
different intersecting layers that make up private practice. A text which will be of
benefit to new practitioners, this book offers a wide-ranging exploration of just how
one can construct the private practice environment within which our work can flour-
ish and also within which our clients can feel safe, contained, and therefore feel met.
There is another layer to this book though. This book also presents some very nuanced
and interesting ideas and exercises regarding how we might use the wider socially
conscious environment to the benefit of our counselling and psychotherapy private
practices. One of the most brilliant parts about this book is the layers of thought that
have gone into the use of different models and the exercises which are attached to
them. It is a book which I would recommend for practitioners to read and also for
courses to add on to their reading lists, so that students and trainees towards the end
of their trainings can have access to this gateway text which opens the door towards
private practice."

Dr Dwight Turner, *Course Leader on the Humanistic Counselling and*
Psychotherapy Course at the University of Brighton, PhD Supervisor at their
Doctoral College, Psychotherapist and Supervisor in private practice

"Finally, a book that captures all the challenges and joys of setting up and running a successful, ethical private practice. It's the book I wish I had when I was setting up my business. Packed full of useful tips, reflections and examples; it is must-read for anyone embarking on, maintaining or supporting others in their private practice. Not only will it benefit those setting up their private practice, it serves as an invaluable tool for the seasoned practitioner wanting to refresh their business. Equally, for supervisors working with supervisees who are venturing into private practice, this book could help you to support them on their journey. Bravo!"

Dr Mish Seabrook, *Resilience Coach, Therapist & Supervisor*

"Neither the beautiful city of Rome nor a successful private practice can (or should) be built in a day. Both take time, skill, patience, and vision. Rome is assembled and standing strong, while Binstead and Sarantakis are here to metaphorically hold your hand as you build your private practice; chapter by chapter; brick by brick. But they don't just want you to build, they want you to build ethically; and not just ethically, but relationally, and that's what makes this book different from the rest. They've thought of everything – so you will too – and guide you every step of the way from graduation, through marketing, contracting, social media and supervision, to ending, all through a three-dimensional lens. If you're ready to build, consider this your foundational brick."

Jeanine Connor, *Psychodynamic Psychotherapist in private practice and author of* 'You're Not My F*cking Mother' and Other Things Gen Z Say in Therapy *(PCCS, 2024),* 'Stop F*cking Nodding' and Other Things 16-year-olds Say in Therapy *(PCCS, 2022) and* Reflective Practice with Children and Adolescents *(Routledge, 2020)*

Relational Ethics in Psychotherapy and Counselling Private Practice

This book explores the ethics around everything connected with setting up and running a therapy private practice.

Offering a hands-on approach to realistic ethical dilemmas encountered by the private practitioner, the book examines the everyday management of practice, and the context of ethical issues in contemporary private practice. Chapters explore the fundamentals of some of the most common ethical considerations in private practice, providing space for the reader to think creatively about how they use their preferred ethical framework, and how that may be translated into an individually tailored approach for each client, and for each private practice. The book provides exercises, examples, and vignettes, in addition to the author's own unique working model, to help the reader bring theoretical reflections into their own everyday practice.

Relational Ethics in Psychotherapy and Counselling Private Practice will help private practitioners feel more confident and grounded in their private practice and up-to-date with developing thoughts. It will also appeal to training institutes, supervisors, and students.

Caz Binstead is an experienced private practitioner, supervisor, and facilitator/visiting lecturer. Specialising in the growth and maintenance of ethical and thriving practice, she was instrumental in the creation of the private practice toolkit at the British Association for Counselling and Psychotherapy (BACP) and acted as divisional lead on the project. Caz is co-lead of the community platform #TherapistsConnect, and was creative director on their two-day conference, "Private practice 2021: surviving and thriving in uncertain times". Through her extensive work in this area, Caz has helped hundreds of therapists with their private practices.

Nicholas Sarantakis is a practising counselling psychologist and couple, family, and group therapist in London and Milton Keynes. He is the author of several academic and professional articles in psychology and psychotherapy. He has taught at five UK universities as Senior Lecturer and Director of Studies. www.nicholassarantakis.com

Ethics in Action: Innovating Ethics in the Counselling Professions

Series Editors: Professor Lynne Gabriel and Professor Andrew Reeves

Series Description:

Ethical relating and working are at the core of the counselling professions. This series provides pragmatic resources in ethics for practitioners in the psychological professions, including counsellors, psychotherapists, counselling psychologists, practitioner trainers, supervisors and researchers; both trainee and trained. The books feature accessible and pragmatic resources on ethics in applied practice across a range of counselling and therapeutic contexts that will assist readers in decision-making in daily practice. The series aims to support meaning-making and ethical decision-making, providing responses for practitioners to key practice questions including "so what does this mean in practice for me, working in this context, with this client group?"

Books in Series:

Navigating Relational Ethics in Day-to-Day Practice: Working Ethically in the Counselling Professions
by Lynne Gabriel and Andrew Reeves

Relational Ethics in Psychotherapy and Counselling Private Practice: Solidarity, Compassion, Justice
by Caz Binstead and Nicholas Sarantakis

Relational Ethics in Psychotherapy and Counselling Private Practice

Solidarity, Compassion, Justice

Caz Binstead and
Nicholas Sarantakis

Routledge
Taylor & Francis Group

LONDON AND NEW YORK

Designed cover image: Getty Images

First published 2025
by Routledge
4 Park Square, Milton Park, Abingdon, Oxon OX14 4RN

and by Routledge
605 Third Avenue, New York, NY 10158

Routledge is an imprint of the Taylor & Francis Group, an informa business

British Library Cataloguing-in-Publication Data
A catalogue record for this book is available from the British Library

ISBN: 978-1-032-56458-6 (hbk)
ISBN: 978-1-032-56459-3 (pbk)
ISBN: 978-1-003-43562-4 (ebk)

DOI: 10.4324/9781003435624

Typeset in Times New Roman
by Newgen Publishing UK

I dedicate this book to all the special people and close friends, who remind me constantly of what it is to be loved, and bring so many of the relational qualities that I hold dear to therapy, into my own life (you know who you are). To my supervisors, Elizabeth and Paul, whose insight, challenge, and unwavering support and compassion, has helped to make me the practitioner I am today. And, a special shout-out to my mum, Claire, who did all she could for us growing up, despite enduring hardship. I surely learnt in my childhood, the importance of challenging injustices; the value of diligence and conscientiousness; and the preciousness of bringing your own shining self into the world.

Caz Binstead

To my loving wife Avis and my precious daughter Katlin, my mother Catherine, brother Anthony and his wife, Anna.

Nicholas Sarantakis

Contents

Acknowledgements

This book would not be possible without the kind souls in our respective lives, who have shown us care, patience, and support. We thank you and dedicate this book to you.

We also appreciate our professional connections. Values we associate with ethics are evident in so many of the wonderful therapists within the community of private practitioners, and have inspired and helped shape this book. Special thanks particularly go to our contributors. Private practitioners deserve to be supported and recognised for their amazing work – we see you.

As authors, we share an appreciation for the great philosophers and spiritual teachers throughout the ages, whose wisdom has touched and inspired us, and helped inform our own musings on the subject of ethics.

Special thanks are extended to Caz's past colleagues in the Private Practice division at the British Association for Counselling and Psychotherapy (BACP). Thank you for believing in the work of the Private practice toolkit, and for backing the rationale for this project, as well as the unique ideas embedded in the work; many of which are extended and celebrated in this book. Especially, to Lesley Ludlow (ex-divisional Chair), and BACP staff member Adam Pollard (who definitely deserved his promotion)! Also, to Rima Sidhpara, who later became Chair, but more importantly, has been a constant friend.

#TherapistsConnect deserves a mention here too. This online community, like others, grew in the difficulties of the pandemic period, and became a source of support for many practitioners, particularly those in the private sector who – as we talk about in this book – are so often isolated (much more so, during this challenging time). It has been a pleasure for Caz to be co-lead alongside Dr Peter Blundell. The journey we have been on, has been one only we will understand. May we always hold space, and advocate, for all dedicated practitioners, regardless of who they are, what status they hold, or sphere they belong to.

Big thanks to our series editors, Professor Lynne Gabriel OBE and Professor Andrew Reeves, for giving us the opportunity to be authors in what will undoubtedly be a valuable series. Also, the peer reviewers who encouraged and supported the work, and our endorsers, who we humbly thank – we value each and every one for their own significant contributions to our field. And, all at Routledge, who have assisted and transformed our words into an actual book!

Finally, we have both undoubtedly learnt the most from our clients. The work we do is special beyond words, and although the people we have worked with over many years remain confidential behind the doors of our own therapy spaces, they remain in our minds and hearts.

Caz Binstead and Nicholas Sarantakis

Chapter 1

The rationale for this book, and an introduction to the three-dimensional model

Caz Binstead and Nicholas Sarantakis

Introduction

Welcome to 21st-century private practice! If you are reading this book, it means you are either already working in the sector, or thinking about embarking on a career as a private practitioner. And you wouldn't be alone – the number of practitioners working in private practice is at an all-time high. The British Association for Counselling and Psychotherapy (BACP) provided their most up-to-date information in figures collected from their Workforce Mapping Survey between October 2021–September 2022. This showed that 69.26% worked in private practice *in some capacity*, with 45.02% stating that it was their primary role, topping both lists as the most common professional role (BACP, 2023). This confirms a general assumption about the continuing exponential rise in this sector, and the need for adequate resource-based support, for, particularly, new private practitioners (Binstead, 2023a).

The authors, Caz, an integrative PSA (Professional Standards Authority) registered counsellor/psychotherapist, and Nicholas, a pluralistic, HCPC (Health and Care Professionals Council) registered counselling psychologist, are committed to offering support, guidance, and confidence building, to all private practitioners. Whether you are an eager student looking ahead, someone new to private practice, or a seasoned practitioner, this book – which explores the ethics around everything connected with setting up and running a therapy practice – brings a contemporary view of the world of private practice, and offers a "hands-on" approach to realistic ethical dilemmas and reflections for the modern-day practitioner.

The niche world of the private practitioner

Given the term "private practice" can sometimes feel wide-reaching, we wish to be clear on our own definition of a private practice for the purposes of this

DOI: 10.4324/9781003435624-1

specific book. We define it as: a business, run by an individual therapist, who creates their own contract, which they communicate with the client (verbal or written). This means a practitioner who holds full responsibility and control of their practice. Although this largely applies to therapists who are sole business owners, we are aware of the complexities and "grey areas", such as where private practitioners form arrangements with others, for example being part of a referral system with a third party, EAP (Employee Assistance Programme) work, group practices, associate arrangements, and so on. We seek to touch on some of the ethical considerations around these types of agreements.

Most private practitioners align explicitly with a specific ethics code of their professional body. However, there is inevitably a gap between generic ethical guidelines (and other mediums, containing theoretical reflections), and hands-on private practice. Ethics codes allow flexibility in the way private practitioners apply their guidelines, because understandably, ethical decision-making, when done effectively, requires an individualised approach (BACP, 2018). This can though, for reasons we'll explore, be challenging for the lone working private practitioner. Furthermore, ethical codes may have other limitations for the 21st-century private practitioner, when it comes to their specific requirements, that is, the ethics of setting up, building, and working in their unique, individual private practices. This book invites a much-needed space for open reflection, with a "bottom-up" practice-based approach.

In writing this book, we are also interested in changes that have been caused by the arrival of COVID-19, in 2020 (as well as connected events, such as the national lockdowns); namely, adaptations that private practitioners were forced to make to their practices during that time. This raised ethical dilemmas that we have never seen before and challenged us to re-think our conventional ways of "doing" therapy. We have devoted a whole chapter to the growth and prevalence of online working, and, have looked at the development of online fora where private practitioners, in the absence of in-person meet-ups, have more readily begun to connect and share. We are curious about what effect this has on a private practitioner's overall general sense of isolation, especially with what appears to be a noticeable rise on social media in open discussions around therapeutic practice and ethical issues. This seems to show a growing desire for an exchange of thoughts between private practitioners and suggests an expanding need for potentially more types of informal peer-support. We look at the potential challenges, benefits, and considerations for therapists around this, as well as looking at the types of supervision spaces, and other support systems, that are on offer for private practitioners.

As relational beings in a world alongside our clients, it has felt important to include themes such as social awareness and social justice. Could therapy be political (in a broad sense)? How do private practitioners work with themes around money, and what are its larger implications for both client and therapist? Do we need to adopt a certain social and online presence in order to be ethical? Is the old-fashioned notion that "the client should know nothing about the therapist" still valid and supported, and what are the contemporary issues around self-disclosure? We also seek to explore how best we can work within a culturally sensitive way with our clients in our individual private practices; one which acknowledges and welcomes the diversity of the human race.

Finally, we will look at the various practicalities of running a private practice, such as the more "business" elements, including administration and marketing. We do so in the context of the "business" being a therapy practice. We anticipate that exploring ethics in a pragmatic, yet strictly confidential way will help support those looking to enter the private practice field, as well as develop and broaden the thinking of seasoned private practitioners. In other words, we hope to increase the confidence of private practitioners in finding ways to reflect on and discuss ethics – in an ethical way!

The three-dimensional model

Throughout this book, we will use composite case studies which are particularly useful for protecting confidentiality (Duffy, 2010), as well hypothetical vignettes, to help you as the reader consider and reflect on ethical dilemmas and scenarios that will come up in your practice, in a safe and confidential way. To be able to look at these in an in-depth way, we have created a working model, known as the three-dimensional model, that we hope may be of benefit to practitioners in enhancing their ethical decision-making skills. This model is based on three dimensions: the client, the private practitioner (including their business), and the wider context and society (we define society as society at large, as well as the societal microcosm of the therapist community). Although we deem the client to always be at the heart of our work, which is backed up by important notions included within frameworks such as, "making clients our primary concern while we are working with them" (BACP, 2018), it would be misleading to suggest that the needs of the private practice business owner does not in some way come into the mix when it comes to private practice. Controversial as this may be to say out loud, we know that, in reality, there is sometimes a conflict between the various dimensions of private practice (Binstead, 2022). And of course, it is also necessary to consider the practice set-ups and boundaries of each unique private practitioner and their business. Furthermore, when we include considerations that a therapist may hold regarding larger societal issues, we allow levels of reflection that could present information that we may not otherwise realise is playing out. Our model, therefore, is a way of advancing our engagement with ethics, beyond simply just our respective ethical codes. In fact, it seeks to elevate our use of these codes, and encourage us through deep reflection, to be more realistic and open to our whole process.

Although we recommend readers to be flexible in how they apply this model (which we demonstrate throughout the book), here's a short case study showing how we might consider all three dimensions:

Case study: Hussein is a recently qualified therapist, who has been working in private practice for five months. He lives and works in the same place: a small, rural area. One night, he attends a local restaurant with his girlfriend, and while she is using the bathroom, her phone receives a notification, and he inadvertently sees the first part of a message flash up. It leads to him to become suspicious that his partner is having an affair, and when she comes back to the table, a row breaks out between them. As tensions rise, voices are raised, and it is only then that he realises that a client of his is sitting on the opposite side of the restaurant. They are looking over, but he is unsure if they have heard, although he thinks that they may have recognised him. He is embarrassed, so quickly asks for the bill, and leaves. Later that evening, he sits thinking about if his client had indeed clocked what was happening, and feels worried about what they might think.

Let's look at this one, by breaking down what might come up in each of the three dimensions.

Focus on the **client**: First and foremost, it feels right that Hussein is concerned about what his client thinks – this means that he has centred his client and their feelings in this situation (BACP, 2018). In order for Hussein to, as suggested by HCPC (HCPC, 2023), "respect and uphold the rights, dignity, values and autonomy" of his client, it is important that he can be open to the client's response to the situation (if indeed they did recognise him and see what was happening). Being open and transparent (BACP, 2018) with his client, in the next session, would demonstrate that he was being attentive and empathic to the client's feelings. It's important to remember that although some clients may not care if they saw their therapist arguing with another, some clients might feel the exact opposite. Anything that could cause hurt to clients needs to be carefully addressed (Binstead, 2023b), especially if the client has not been given an active choice around working with a therapist who lives and practices in the same place. Hussein would need to reflect on if he has contracted well enough with his client to have made this information clear to them.

Focus on the **private practitioner**: It is crucial that Hussein can reflect on his feelings. Worry and panic can sometimes lead to premature and potentially unwise actions, such as emailing clients in-between sessions. It's important that Hussein can hold his boundaries and contain himself, and that any actions come from an intention around what feels best for the client. Another possibility is that Hussein may feel that as this is his private life, and does not concern his clients, he does not have to bring it up in their next session. He might also choose this option by "hoping for the best" that is, that the client did not realise what was going on. If he doesn't bring it up, though, could it become an "elephant in the room", possibly affecting the work as well as their relationship (if the client felt Hussein didn't care about his feelings)? This might also risk something unspoken, such as a loss of confidence in Hussein as a therapist. It's worth remembering that therapists are human too, and so of course have the right to become upset in our private lives. It feels important for Hussein to honour **both** his worry about the client and his own uncomfortableness with the situation, especially as the example implies it is an isolated incident.

Focus on wider **societal context** – here's some questions to consider:

- In our responsibilities of upholding the integrity of our profession, does this include rowing with our partners in public?
- Given inadvertent self-disclosures may run further than the example given, how much of an active life do we as a profession allow therapists who work and live in the same area? If there are restrictions on this, we might question how fair this is. Especially when you compare it to the

active life of a therapist who lives and works in different areas. And what about potential discrimination in this? For example, if a therapist chooses to do this because they cannot afford commuter fees. We also might consider the general ethics of placing an expectation on therapists to construct their lives in a more managed, and potentially restrictive way, which is wholly dependent on factors such as the location of their home – like for Hussein, who lives in a smaller, rural area, where the likelihood of bumping into clients is greater.

- If we name Hussein's actions as "unethical", what message does it send to our clients and wider society? Is there an unspoken assumption that we as therapists portray ourselves as something above humanity, and that we "shouldn't" ever have an unfortunate incident happen?

Conclusion: On balance, the authors feel that, assuming there are no further developments (and Hussein and his client are meeting as usual), it would be useful for Hussein to be transparent. To do so would be a good demonstration of relational therapy – relational towards his client and their feelings, as well as showing his own humanness in accepting that sometimes things happen which are unusual and out of the blue. There are some further questions he might like to consider, such as how the conversation might go, and what the intention for the focus of it will be, including the ethical implications around any possible further self-disclosure (such as giving an in-depth explanation). Balancing attending to the needs or worries of the client, and the larger context of what has happened between them relationally, without feeling he needs to give an "explanation" with all the details, feels like a good approach. Broadly speaking as therapists, we do need to prepare for such scenarios, so Hussein would do well to reflect in supervision about if he has engaged with his clients in the contracting stage over the possibility of bumping into them, which, given he lives/works in a smaller, rural area, makes the likelihood greater. And, reflect further on how to manage being a therapist who lives and works in the same area – what does he view as acceptable or not; what other areas of his life might be affected by this; and how does he negotiate the implications of a client seeing him outside of the therapy room, without him feeling overly restricted. Finally, if we accept this scenario as not ideal, it feels appropriate for Hussein to reflect on and learn from this experience, and consider what, if anything, he might do differently next time.

*Please note:

- Throughout the book, we will use the words "therapist", "private practitioner", or "practitioner" to refer to qualified psychotherapists, counsellors, and counselling psychologists (or other practitioner psychologists) working within this field.
- As integrative/pluralistic therapists, at times we refer to the concept of transference and countertransference (in line with Petruska Clarkson's five relationship model[1]). We recognise that not everyone will use this language, and/or work with transference. In terms of relational practice, we hope all readers, regardless of their modality, can be curious in general about the benefits of bringing into their awareness any relational dynamics that may be happening in the room (as part of their own process of reflexivity).
- This book can either be read from start to finish in one, or by dipping in and out of the chapters. Our first chapter, which is aimed at students, might be skimmed over by the seasoned private practitioner, or you might find that it provides fresh ideas for developing private practice. Find what works for you!

Note

1 Petruska Clarkson outlined her relational model in her book, *The Therapeutic Relationship*. The five components are as follows: 1. The Working Alliance; 2. The Transferential/Countertransferential Relationship; 3. The Reparative/ Developmentally Needed Relationship; 4. The I-You Relationship/Person-Person Relationship; 5. The Transpersonal Relationship.

References

BACP (British Association for Counselling & Psychotherapy) (2018). *Ethical framework for the counselling professions*. BACP. www.bacp.co.uk/media/3103/bacp-ethical-framework-for-the-counselling-professions-2018.pdf

BACP (2023). 2021–2022 Workplace mapping survey: News for members. BACP. www.bacp.co.uk/about-us/about-bacp/2021-2022-workplace-mapping-survey/

Binstead, C. (2022). *Negotiation of the business with ethical, therapeutic practice*. BACP. www.bacp.co.uk/bacp-divisions/bacp-private-practice/private-practice-tool kit/negotiation-of-the-business-with-ethical-therapeutic-practice/

Binstead, C. (2023a). *Student to private practice, use of the BACP toolkit*. Presentation delivered at the 2021 BACP student conference. BACP. www.bacp.co.uk/bacp-divisions/bacp-private-practice/private-practice-toolkit/setting-up-your-private-practice/

Binstead, C. (2023b). *An isolated sector: Thinking about holistic self-care in private practice*. [Workshop session]. Onlinevents. https://onlinevents.co.uk/courses/an-isolated-sector-thinking-about-holistic-self-care-in-private-practice-workshop-with-caz-binstead/

Duffy, M. (2010). Writing about clients: Developing composite case material and its rationale. *Counseling and Values*, 54(2), 135–153. doi: 10.1002/j.2161-007X.2010.tb00011.x.

HCPC (Health and Care Professions Council) (2023). *Practitioner psychologists: The standards of proficiency for practitioner psychologists*. HCPC. www.hcpc-uk.org/standards/standards-of-proficiency/practitioner-psychologists/

Chapter 2

Initial ethical considerations into transitioning from being a student to a private practitioner

Caz Binstead and Nicholas Sarantakis

A bit of background

"I've just qualified, and want to go into private practice – how, and where do I start?" The question littered all over social media these days! And of course, there are very good reasons for this. Many students leave their trainings ill-equipped to set up in private practice (Binstead, 2022a), and yet, as stated in Chapter 1, almost 70% of BACP members are in fact working in some capacity in the field. The rise in this is almost certainly connected to the lack of paid jobs, particularly in the counselling and psychotherapy profession. Jo Langston (the former ethics services manager at BACP) and author Caz Binstead, who at the time was Private Practice divisional lead of the *Private practice toolkit* at BACP, chatted with the popular student social media platform Counselling Tutor in 2020 about the reason for the creation of the toolkit; the former confirming the BACP's view at the time, that paid job opportunities were not as forthcoming as they once had been (Lees-Oakes & Kelly, 2023). Furthermore, there are suggestions that historic systems operating within our profession essentially create barriers to therapists obtaining paid employment (CTUK, 2021). With anecdotal evidence indicating that there is a change in the age demographic of those training to be therapists though, expectations from a new generation around being paid for their work will undoubtably be higher. This, in contrast to data provided in a *Therapy Today* article, entitled *Is counselling women's work*. Using information obtained from a 2014 BACP survey of its membership, the article discussed how our profession is overrun by females (84%), with a typical age of 53, and that in marketing terms, this typical therapist "falls into the 'affluent achiever' bracket" (Brown, 2017). In other words, someone who may not necessarily *need* to earn a living. Times have certainly changed, and let's face it, if the counselling and psychotherapy professions wish to present themselves as a legitimate industry, then it should

DOI: 10.4324/9781003435624-2

not be unusual for therapists to a) wish to undertake work in the field in which they have been trained, b) earn a wage from this, and c) be properly supported in working in a unique sector (such as private practice).

Within therapy networks, it is noticeable that particularly new private practitioners get very invested in growing their businesses, and seek out consultants or online training courses in building a "successful" practice (Binstead, 2023a). In fact, the number of courses in this area that have popped up in recent years follow the trend of growth in the field of private practice. The only problem being that literally anyone could set up a course, and there is a lot of money to be made in this area; especially considering the nervousness of so many new private practitioners. In which case, despite there being many sound and valuable private practice experts providing services, we may question the ethics of our profession relying on such methods to fulfil the shortfall in proper trainings. Binstead, who identifies as a relational activist (Dove & Fisher, 2019), outlined in 2020 on the *#TherapistsConnect* podcast (Blundell & Binstead, 2023) her quest to endeavour to "fill this gap", and be a part of providing adequate support within a more appropriate place, namely, a Professional Standards Authority (PSA) regulated membership body. The aim being to help the thousands of private practitioners who suffered from the job shortfall, some of whom desperately needed to earn a living. But despite the creation of the Private practice toolkit at BACP, there is still much work to be done across the board in recognising the unique needs of this sector. This is especially with regards to ethics, and keeping clients safe, as well as in helping the community of private practitioners, who, due to the nature of this isolated sector, are particularly vulnerable to difficulty and complaints. Both authors, in upholding the value and substance of the words within our subtitle, "Solidarity, Compassion, Justice", continue this supportive and developmental work.

Thinking about becoming a private practitioner

Being a private practitioner is in many ways a wonderful life! You get to do what you've been studying to do for years, and you can earn a decent living (that's right, it's okay to want that!). Other benefits are that you have complete autonomy over your own practice; you can choose your own hours and create your own schedule; you can explore niche areas of interest to focus on/specialise in, and, if you have your own space to work in, have the pleasure of creating your very own consulting room in line with the therapist you are. Furthermore, you can consider working in the same place that you live (if it seems viable for your business), meaning less time and money on commuting, and introduce whatever resources you see fit to your practice (this may even include "resources" like animals, such as a therapy dog)! You might also enjoy the freedom of exploring the different ways of conducting therapy, for example, online therapy, hybrid therapy, outdoor therapy. And of course, you can make changes to things as you progress along in your career, so there's a degree of flexibility that you may not get with a paid role. The possibilities with private practice are endless, and the good news is that apart from a few basics, which constitute what is known as "collective knowledge" (Binstead, 2020), there are no static rules. But so many private practitioners can feel paralysed by starting the process, and sometimes even more so, in continuing the process beyond any arising challenges.

Look at the following questions/worries, do any of them resonate with you?

- How long does it take to get established in private practice?
- Where will I work, and how do I go about deciding this?
- Am I qualified enough?
- I feel like I'm an imposter.
- What if I don't get clients?
- My friend seems to know what she's doing, but I have no idea where to start.
- I'm ambivalent about charging clients for therapy.
- What are the differences between my own private practice, and EAP (Employment Assistant Programme) work?
- I'm not very good at administration.
- Business?! I'm not a businessperson, I'm a therapist!
- I feel scared to make the jump into private practice – what if it doesn't work out?

Having questions, and being uncertain of something new, is entirely normal. In some ways, it would be more worrying if you were not reflecting on how you might find this journey. First, and foremost, hear this – you absolutely can build a thriving private practice, as shown by the many therapists who have enjoyed long careers as private practitioners.

Getting started – the road to private practice

The reality is that private practice starts with just one client. One client, and you have a private practice! Imagine that moment … you don't want to miss it. It will be the start of something that you might want to do for the rest of your career. Although it's understandable to worry about how we might find the experience of developing our private practice, we don't need to get hung up on where we're going, thinking about where we want to be, and how fast our practice is going to grow. Of course, there may be real-life circumstances that could be dictating this, such as the need to earn a living, but let's also have a reality check, and remember, Rome was not built in a day! And if it had been, it wouldn't have been quite as beautiful as it is. Often, the first errors that private practitioners make is expecting to have a ground-breaking, "successful" business as soon as they start, or even as soon as they qualify as a therapist. But this book demonstrates just how many considerations there are in running a private practice, and that it is not abnormal for it take a few months to get up and running properly. Factored into that, too, is the all-important preparation time, and if you are currently in the latter stages of your training, this is something you can start now. Of course, there is nothing wrong with ambition, and we can have *intentions* about where we want to be, but engaging in committed reflexivity in our preparation (which is an essential part of ethical practice) means our feet need to be deeply rooted in the present moment. So, let's start that now. In both our introduction, and the beginning of this chapter, we set out some background to the rationale for this book, partly because some of it has a direct effect on a new private practitioner's experience. Reflect on this question – do you actually want to go into private practice, or do you feel you have to, in order to earn a living? The differences between those two things mean there will be differences in how a person will psychologically feel in building their practice. And being curious about how we psychologically feel about it, and responding to that, marks the start of your individualised process of becoming a private practitioner. Your unique journey is something we'll keep coming back to in this book.

> Those who stand on tiptoe
> do not stand firm
> Those who rush ahead
> don't get very far.
> *Tao Te Ching*
> (Lao-Tzu, 1996)

Preparation

If you're reading this book as a student transitioning to private practice, or you're generally new to the sector, then you have already begun your preparation. Each of these chapters cover areas that are known to require multi-faceted considerations, around ethical practice. If you skim the chapter headings, certain words may spring out at you – "contract", "marketing", and so on. Before jumping to how you can actively do these things, it can be useful to start by thinking about *how* these words make you feel? If we take the two above, maybe it evokes panic? Or maybe you instantly feel confident. Whatever, tuning into your feelings around different elements of private practice can be helpful in this preparation stage. To do so is to acknowledge that the journey to private practice is likely to be a mixed bag for many of us, because different parts require different skills. An honesty with oneself in the first instance about what parts we may find easier, and what parts we may find more challenging is important for ethical practice. Because if we skip over some of the things we find more difficult, or don't afford ourselves the space to think about how we might go about working with those parts, we are more likely to make ethical mistakes. Unfortunately, we cannot avoid every eventuality, and mistakes afterall are part of life, but the more active reflection we can do, the greater the chance we can slowly work through and evaluate how we're doing in the various aspects of running a private practice.

This case study below shows Martin engaging in some early reflective preparation:

Case study: Martin, who is four months away from finishing his therapy training, has begun to think about private practice. He makes some notes, where he splits things that he has to consider into themes, and then splits them further into certain skill sets. He begins with marketing because it is one he finds easier to reflect on as he has some experience in marketing from a previous role. He figures that these are transferable skills, so will be useful to get him started on the basics. But he's also aware that marketing a therapy business probably requires different considerations to marketing within a more generalised service industry, especially when thinking about ethical practice. He makes a note that he needs to think further about this and try and do some reading/research to drill down on the similarities and the differences.

Martin has the right idea here, as he is utilising the knowledge he already has. Like many, he had been quite nervous when thinking about getting started, but this has helped his imposter syndrome to lessen. Being gentle and kind with yourself will enable you to feel less overwhelmed, and create better conditions for building your confidence in the things you have less experience in.

Exercise

Have a go at completing the following statements.
   When thinking about setting up in private practice:

- I feel excited about …
- I feel nervous about …
- I feel confident about …

A closer look at ethics in private practice

Another reason why reflection is such an important skill in private practice is because a private practice is both a therapy practice, AND a business. Private practitioners need to carefully balance these two dynamics, while also accepting the reality that there will sometimes be tension between them (Binstead, 2022b). This can be a challenge for several reasons. Building our own practice takes time and effort, and sometimes there is a natural desire to make decisions that perhaps on the business side of things make sense, even though it might compromise ethical therapeutic practice. A lot of ethical dilemmas that we look at in this book revolve around some of these rubs, and the more honest we can be about them, the more we can bring them to the surface and work through them (including identifying any internal barriers).

The other major challenge for a new private practitioner is described by one of the authors, Caz:

The biggest difference with private practice is the lack of direct support available. When working within placements or agencies, we often have a "scaffolding structure" around us as therapists. So, there may well be a number of people holding different roles to whom we can refer if stuck, or, when faced with an ethical dilemma, for example, an in-house supervisor, a placement manager, a clinical manager, a head of services, and so forth. A structured organisation is also likely to have in-house policies and procedures in terms of practice management and contracting. And so entering the private practice sector, can really highlight the isolation of a sole-trader therapy business, whilst also laying bare the responsibilities that come with building and maintaining a practice.

(Binstead, 2022c)

What this means is that part of the trickiness of setting up and adjusting to working within a private practice is not just about managing the various elements of running a private practice but also learning how to handle the responsibility (and potential pressure), bound up in the process of ethical decision-making.

Ethics in action

Case Study: George has recently opened his private practice and is receiving a lot of enquiries. Eager to grow his practice, he starts booking clients in, but hasn't given that much thought to when he *wants* to work. Very soon, he has clients scattered throughout the day, on five consecutive working days. He very quickly begins to feel tired, to the point where he is finding it difficult to stay focussed with his clients.

George's ambition to grow his practice has directly impacted his client work in a negative way. This is a good example of how even one of the benefits of being a self-employed private practitioner – the freedom to set your own schedule – can create a potential conflict with the practice of ethical therapy.

Exercise

Work through the points below, and see if you can positively embrace the ability to choose your own schedule, while being mindful and reflective of the responsibilities of being an ethical therapist:

- Be curious about what kind of person you are. Are you more an early bird, or a night-owl? This might inform when you work.
- How many clients are you currently seeing in a row? How does that feel for you? Can you envisage what any more in a day might feel like?
- How energetic are you throughout the day? Is your energy consistent, or do you have moments when it dips, or peters out?

- What are your current eating habits? Many private practitioners who work evenings needs to think about this, as they may be working through what is usually their dinner time. What are your thoughts on this – would you set aside an hour in the evening in-between clients to eat, or eat when you have finished (even if later)? Or, would you eat smaller portions or snacks in-between clients as you go?
- Does it suit you better to have set-slots? Or, if you want to be more flexible, are you disciplined with yourself in how many clients you are taking on at any given time?
- How does it feel to say "no" to a client who asks to come at a less desirable time?

Choosing where you work

Giving proper thought as to where you work as a private practitioner is an important part of the preparation stage. Private practitioners may choose to work in their own rented stand-alone consulting room, while many others see clients within their own home, either in-person, online (see Chapter 6), or as part of a blended mode of delivery. And there is also the option to work from an established counselling centre or psychology clinic. With the latter, it is important to be aware that what this looks like in practice can differ, depending on where you are working, and what arrangements are stated in the mutual agreement between the parties. In our introduction, we declare that for the purposes of this book, we define a private practitioner as someone who establishes their own contract, and has responsibility for their own business. Yet across the world, there are many "hybrid" options, such as certain group practice arrangements, seen largely in the USA, and the popular practice in the UK of existing private therapy services taking on a therapist (who would routinely identify as a private practitioner) as a "clinical associate". The advantages to working within established businesses may range from sophisticated online marketing, thereby saving the therapist time and money; administrative services which take care of things like invoices; rooms in ideal locations, and perhaps most importantly, a referral service. In fact, some private practitioners will choose to work with third parties where they are working independently in every other way, but are part of a formal referral network. The downsides to any of these arrangements might be that you must follow certain protocols, such as set "assessment" arrangements (see Chapter 3); that there is sometimes encouragement of "after-care" feed-back/testimonials from clients, which raises some ethical questions (see Chapter 4); that you may need to share a portion of your fees to cover services offered, and that even professional arrangements that might feel a lot looser in general, such as referral networks, could have caveats written into their agreements which have implications, and yet are sometimes easy to miss. It can be hard to practice ethically, if we are unsure of how much responsibility we have over our businesses, and also if we have conflicting values, needs, or philosophy of practice than that aligned with the service. Therefore, being aware of all the protocols and the associated boundaries that come with any agreement is paramount. To research more on where you might work, we recommend reading *Setting Up and Running a Therapy Business* (Rye, 2017), or a resource from Caz, entitled *Location and Place of Work* www.bacp.co.uk/bacp-divisions/bacp-private-practice/private-practice-toolkit/location-and-place-of-work/ (which BACP members can read for free).

Mind-set

While many new private practitioners, particularly those who feel exceptionally nervous, like to soak up the wisdom of those who consult or advise in the field of private practice, in fact internal confidence is one of the things that is going to benefit you as a private practitioner. Confidence is all about trusting yourself and your abilities, and is what allows us to embrace things that come part and parcel with private practice, such as elements of the unknown, the need to some-times take risks, and to not shy away from sitting through challenging times. While we might be all unique in our make-up, and certainly confidence will come more naturally to some people than others, to be able to maintain ethical practice we need to feel comfortable floating with the uncertainties of private practice. Caz suggests a concept she calls the "known supporting the unknown" (Binstead, 2020), where we can be more at ease with that which we don't have so much control over, by resting in the supportive structures that we have built around us. Some of these certainties can be the learning and self-reflection done in aid of becoming a private practitioner – the knowledge you have about yourself and who you are; the people and systems you have in place to help you; the collective wisdom from an "expert" or the community of private practitioners, and so on. And some of it can be found intrinsically in you, through your own discovery of self-knowledge (Binstead, 2023).

Exercise

Have a look at the list below, and see if you identify with any of the statements:

- Jasreen currently has a paid role but wants to move into private practice. However, she is nervous to commit. She worries about her ability to ride the waves of uncertainty which comes with growing a business, so continues to spend lots of money on workshops in private practice, hoping she will eventually be knowledgeable enough to make the leap.
- Deliah is a nervous therapist, and although she sets boundaries in her practice, she finds it hard to stick to them when working with clients.
- Jack has heard that it's good to develop a niche. However, he worries that he isn't really specialised enough in anything, so decides to instead stick to "general therapy".
- Melchia believes that their personality just does not fit with being a businessperson or having an interest in marketing. They also find the thought of being active on social media very restrictive and boring.
- Janet wants to go into private practice, but just doesn't feel good enough, as a therapist. She feels she needs more experience.
- Malcom wants to make a living out of private practice but doesn't feel comfortable setting a fee that allows him to live comfortably.

These therapists could, if they wanted to, take the time to work through these common worries. As private practitioners there may well be a range of things we feel nervous about, and some are barriers that would need working on to succeed in running an ethical practice. But, if we can individualise *how* we relate to certain aspects of private practice, we can work out what we need development in, and how we can grow in confidence in the unique qualities we already have. The more settled, reflective, and grounded a private practitioner is, the better it will be for our clients.

It is of course worth saying, and hopefully obvious, that although confidence is an essential part of private practice, and helps maintain ethical practice, over-confidence, or complacency, is likely to do the opposite, as it will probably restrict self-reflection.

Deepening our thinking about private practice

One of the things that students and those new to private practice are perhaps not told enough is to imagine a way of running your practice that elicits enjoyment and satisfaction. Rumi, the great philosopher and poet said: "when you do things from your soul, you feel a river moving in you, a joy" (as cited in Barks, 2002), and there is certainly something to be said about finding the place within you, where you can move at ease, and connect with your practice, with a felt-sense of your internal being – the very depths of who you are. In other words, we are not doing it to conquer a challenge, or embroiled in the "task" of improving our confidence, but simply for the love of who we are, and what we can bring to a private practice. Bruce Lee, the well-known martial artist, who considered himself a student of philosophy and life, said: "always be yourself, express yourself, have faith in yourself. Do not go out and look for a successful personality and duplicate it" (Lee, as cited in Little, 1996). This quote says so much in terms of what makes a thriving practice. The word "success" itself can sometimes be a red herring, because one person's success does not make another's. Also, because success is not a cloak that can be worn – an external covering that constitutes all the elements of the quintessential "private practitioner super-hero"! There is something important to be said about creating our own values in our practices and living them. It's much more likely to inspire us and make us proud of what we do.

Finding ourselves and holding our own space is a crucial element of private practice. Not only are we battling our own levels of self-belief, including comparisons with other private practitioners, but in areas of the UK certainly we are also living in a culture of high expectations. This is where society may have a direct impact on some of our clients, placing certain expectations on the therapy space, particularly when clients are paying for their therapy. As relational practitioners, we need to be acutely aware of our own personal triggers. In this example, there is a transferential process happening in the room, but we will see that Paddy fails to notice it, because he goes back in his mind, to a self-belief that he is not good enough.

Ethics in action

> **Case study**: Paddy, a therapist who has been in private practice for six months, has taken great pride in setting up his private practice. He likes to have everything as perfect as he can, and sometimes even hides the worries that he has about his practice from his supervisor, because he doesn't want them to think he is incompetent. He is working with Jerry, who originally presented with difficulties around anxiety, self-worth,

and feelings of inadequacy. On the seventh session, Paddy began to feel like he was failing Jerry, when halfway through the session Jerry started to question the productiveness of the therapy. Paddy was embarrassed and began to "try harder". He talked for most of the remainder of the session, ensuring there were no silences. Once the session ended, he began to plan what work they could do together for the next few sessions. He felt he had failed Jerry and needed to do better as a therapist. He also felt deep down that he was failing at his private practice, and that clients might start to end with him.

Analysis: As a therapist reading from the outside, we might reflect on how much this feeling of inadequacy is due to Paddy's short-comings, or due to something else that Jerry is bringing into the room. Transference has been defined as "the client's experience of the therapist that is shaped by his or her own psychological structures and the past" (Gelso & Hayes, 1998, p. 11), and we might call this a potential "projective identification" and counter-transferential response. This would be where feelings that the client cannot manage (or are unacceptable to self) are unconsciously projected onto the therapist (Waska, 1999). Given we know Paddy already has similar issues, then like Velcro, it might make it easier for something that belongs to another but gets projected onto them to "stick". Paddy might do well to consider if he felt a sudden feeling of pressure, and to be open-minded about if he really needed to address his way of working, or, if it might serve Jerry better therapeutically, to instead do the opposite; perhaps by slowing down and putting the focus back on him and his own issues around self-worth. It's not always clearcut what is happening in the therapy space, and we don't know the actual answer here, but an ethical consideration is whether Paddy will take it to his supervisor (or, peer supervision) to get further perspectives. If he doesn't, he could become very stuck in his own insecurities, and that will no doubt have a negative impact on his work. At the same time, it might knock his confidence in the long-term about his private practice, and his fears around clients ending with him in general, could "leak" into his other client's spaces. Isn't it amazing how one small comment from a client can open a whole world of possibilities? Being ever present to this will help keep a private practitioner aware of their growing edges, ensure ethical practice, and enhance the therapeutic work.

Other considerations for starting a private practice

Have you also thought about …

- The different types of therapy practices?
- How to keep safe as a lone worker?
- If you will be working as a full-time private practitioner, or part-time. There are similarities and differences between the two, although it is useful to be mindful that the former will potentially place more pressure on maintaining the business, because it might be your only income.
- If you are becoming a full-time private practitioner, what does this mean for you in terms of the number of clients per week that you see? Around 20 might be a sensible upper limit, but the ideal number will differ for each person (and at times may dip or increase, depending on your circumstances).

Working with others – the private practice community

We were talking earlier about how we can balance our own self-learning, reflexivity, and self-belief with learning from others via networking. And so, thinking about how you might create a supportive system from the outset is vital. Students spend so much of their time being with peers – in class, on placement, in supervision groups, and so on – and many mourn the loss of this when they qualify, particularly if they go into private practice and are hit with the shock of an isolated field. We can never get back what we once had, and nor should we be trying as private practitioners to replicate our student experience. However, there is something to be said about the benefits of taking from this, and continuing the basic premise of joint learning and development, albeit in a different way. Students could perhaps identify which of their peers are going into private practice too and agree to keep in touch. Maybe there could be a way of finding a joint space to work from, or to create a group of independent practitioners, with a joint referral network. It's important to draw on who you are as a person, and what may work best for you in terms of "networking". Not everybody will want to create formal ongoing arrangements, and if not, what other options are there? Here's a list of just a few things to consider:

- Could you connect with people via social media? Furthermore, can you support another private practitioner by "liking" and/or sharing their content, to aid in the growth of their business? Will you feel comfortable in asking the same of others? You can read more on the ethical consider- ations, as well as experiences from other private practitioners in our social media chapter (Chapter 11).

- Could you create a list or database of your contemporaries' skills, areas of interest, and intended location of work (including if they will work online)? You can read more about referrals in Chapter 4.
- Can you begin the search for your supervisor, who is a vital part of your experience as a private practitioner (see Chapter 10).
- Can you agree to be a "private practice support friend" – an arrangement where you both will check in on each other, and send mutual messages of support, in an aim to motivate with the task of building a practice.
- Can you leave reviews for others starting out on this journey? Although you clearly wouldn't have been their client, if they have been a classmate, or in a supervision group with you, you may have a good idea of what they are like as a therapist. So long as the boundaries are clear in the review, and there is transparency that you are a therapist (not a client), then this can be a great ethical way to help a contemporary to start to grow their practice.
- Can you set up a regular co-working group, which focuses on *specific* things that would fall outside of peer supervision, for instance in private practice administration, or elements of building your practice. This can help increase motivation, provide support and much needed company via community and friends, and accountability. It could also (alongside your supervisor) help you learn more about your way of working and getting things done as an individual, and help spread knowledge and wisdom between private practitioners in purpose-filled designated spaces.
- Can you re-discover the word "networking" to make it relevant to you? One of the authors despised this word for years because it brought up cer- tain connotations for them connected with the "corporate" world. They reframed it by thinking of it as a simple concept which revolved around the sharing of their authentic self, in chosen spaces where they felt com- fortable. Remember, don't be afraid to embrace your differences!
- Is there anything challenging which you could outsource to others? For instance, could someone do your taxes, or even help create a simple spreadsheet for you. How about getting someone to do your website? Or how about a social media PA? Not a lot of money needs to be spent on private practice, but sometimes if you do have extra resources (even if not

right at the beginning), it can be useful to think about what may make your life easier. And remember, we can make changes within the first year, so if you don't have either the time or the money to have someone help you, can you schedule space for this a few months down the line? This kind of planning can help alleviate any worry or pressure that a private practitioner may be holding. There is a lot to organise and manage in private practice, especially at the beginning, and pressure and being overwhelmed are not conducive to the stress and nerves that may already be there when starting a new business.

- Is there anything else you might want to add?

Private practice: a global sector

Although global therapy practice consists of different standards and regulations, with the advent of social media, private practitioners have been able to communicate and share ideas, relating to practice, in a way unseen before. Private practice is, in essence, a relational business, and this can be seen best in core aspects of the authentic life of a private practitioner. For example, there may not be too much difference between a UK private practitioner and a US private practitioner when it comes to themes such as creating your niche; exploring personal values to establish what your unique private practice looks like; the importance of networking and connection, and certain ways of growing a practice. We are curious throughout this book on how useful ethical codes are to private practitioners specifically, but would argue at this point, that, particularly in this contemporary era, working private practitioners have much wisdom to offer on ethical practice from different corners of the earth – maybe even (controversially) more so than the ethical codes do themselves.

TAKE-AWAY MESSAGES: If you're a student thinking of going into private practice, why not start preparing now? Take your time and enjoy this process of learning. And don't forget ... reflect, reflect, reflect!

References

Barks, C. (2002). *The soul of Rumi: A new collection of ecstatic poems*. HarperOne.

Binstead, C. (2020). Tools of the trade. *Private Practice.* www.bacp.co.uk/bacp-journals/private-practice/september-2020/articles/tools-of-the-trade/

Binstead, C. (2022a). *Student to private practice.* BACP. www.bacp.co.uk/bacp-divisions/bacp-private-practice/private-practice-toolkit/student-to-private-practice/

Binstead, C. (2022b). *Negotiation of the business with ethical, therapeutic practice.* BACP. www.bacp.co.uk/bacp-divisions/bacp-private-practice/private-practice-toolkit/negotiation-of-the-business-with-ethical-therapeutic-practice/

Binstead, C. (2022c). *The buck stops with you.* BACP. www.bacp.co.uk/bacp-divisions/bacp-private-practice/private-practice-toolkit/the-buck-stops-with-you/

Binstead, C. (2023). *Student to private practice, use of the BACP toolkit.* Presentation delivered at the 2021 BACP student conference. BACP. www.bacp.co.uk/bacp-divisions/bacp-private-practice/private-practice-toolkit/setting-up-your-private-practice/

Blundell, P., Binstead, C. (2023). Dr. *Peter Blundell interviews Caz Binstead about her life and work. The #TherapistsConnect Podcast.* www.therapists-connect.com/podcast/episode/498a23b9/caz-binstead

Brown, S. (2017). Is counselling women's work? *Therapy Today,* 28(2), 6–9. www.bacp.co.uk/bacp-journals/therapy-today/2017/march-2017/is-counselling-womens-work/#:~:text=While%20psychotherapy%20is%20rooted%20in,researching%20the%20history%20of%20counselling

CTUK (2021). *The cycle of counsellor exploitation.* https://ukcounsellors.co.uk/wp-content/uploads/2021/04/THE-CYCLE-OF-COUNSELLOR-EXPLOITATION.pdf

Dove, B., Fisher, T. (2019). Becoming unstuck with relational activism. *Stanford Social Innovation Review.* https://ssir.org/articles/entry/becoming_unstuck_with_relational_activism

Gelso, C. J., Hayes, J. A. (1998). *The psychotherapy relationship: Theory, research, and practice.* Wiley.

Lees-Oakes, R., Kelly, K. (2023). *BACP Special: Starting a private practice in counselling. Counselling Tutor Podcast.* https://counsellingtutor.com/starting-a-private-practice-in-counselling

Little, J. (1996). *The philosophies of Bruce Lee.* Chartwell Books.

Rye, J. (2017). *Setting up and running a therapy business: Frequently asked questions.* Routledge.

Tzu, L. (1996). *Tao Te Ching.* https://simplybeing-sw.co.uk/wp-content/uploads/2016/12/Tao-Te-Ching-J.H.-McDonald-1996.pdf. (Complete online text a translation for the public domain by J.H. McDonald.)

Waska, R. (1999). Projective identification, countertransference, and the struggle for understanding over acting out. *Journal of Psychotherapy Practice and Research,* 8(2), 155–161.

Chapter 3

Ethical confidence in our practices

Admin and everyday practice management

Caz Binstead and Nicholas Sarantakis

Your practice – your business! Building a private practice is made up of a lot of different components, and one of the things that private practitioners can struggle with is the intricacies involved. When it comes to practice management, each element enables us to successfully run our business, but in turn, also requires us to reflect on what ethical responsibilities we have towards our clients. In this chapter, we will explore practice management beyond the contract (which we will look at in detail in Chapter 5), focussing on *why* we may include certain things. We will also look at the processes behind this, and how we can make sure we have allocated the time and space that is realistically needed for the admin side of our private practices, being aware that we all as individuals relate to such things in different ways. We will also explore the importance of a private practitioner knowing the difference between legal obligations and ethical considerations, and where this might differ between the counselling professions, that is, the difference between a counselling psychologist, who is HCPC regulated, and a counsellor/psychotherapist.

Practice management

To successfully maintain a private practice, you will need to have a collection of policies and forms – some of which will concern legal requirements; some which are crucial to any ethical private practice and others which are not necessarily essential, but may well be useful for respective private practitioners.

Daisy's paperwork for her private practice

- Assessment paperwork.

DOI: 10.4324/9781003435624-3

- Contact details form. *Note to self*: remember to include details on this, including what method a client would prefer to be contacted, and if by phone, if it is okay to leave a message.
- Contract.
- Clinical will.
- Overview of my General Data Protection Regulation (GDPR) policies, laid out in my privacy notice.
- Emergency situation policy (used previously for Covid, and miscellaneous, from now on).
- Social media policy.
- Note-taking template.
- Risk assessment paperwork.
- Third party referrals.
- Request to share information form.
- Customised reduced fee agreement.
- Receipt/invoice template.
- First aid and accident book.
- Psychotherapeutic resources.
- Financial record systems relating to HMRC tax responsibilities.
- DBS (Disclosure Barring Service).

Exercise

Before reading ahead in the chapter, can you go through Daisy's list and ascertain which falls under which category (E = Essential ethical; L = Essential Legal; O = Optional). To try and work out the essentials, try and imagine what might happen if you didn't have a particular form. Also, be curious at this stage about your knowledge of what constitutes as legal, and what falls under the ethical banner.

In addition to their policy list, Daisy also has a set of reminders for things that will need doing throughout the year.

My reminders

- Renew and pay my Information Commissioner's Office (ICO) data protection fee annually.
- Renew and pay my Professional Civil Liability insurance, which covers Professional Indemnity and Public Liability insurance. Read my new documentation to ensure I keep abreast of any changes I might need to know about.

- Renew my professional body membership annually.
- Keep an eye on the date of renewal for each of my directories.
- Complete my sole trader self-assessment tax return (due in January).

As this a book is focussing on ethics, we are choosing not to go in depth on practical elements around tax and finance, but if you are a BACP member you can view the following document, written by Paul Silver-Meyer, a practising psychotherapist, who is also an accountant, for free: *Understanding tax in the 21ˢᵗ century*. www.bacp.co.uk/bacp-divisions/bacp-private-practice/priv ate-practice-toolkit/understanding-tax-in-the-21st-century/

Initial session paperwork

There are a variety of ways that private practitioners may conduct their initial sessions, mainly based on their modality, and the way they practice. In fact, we refer to it as either the "initial session" or "assessment" as the language around this can really matter to some practitioners. On a practical basis though, there are, in general, some basic things that could be useful to include on any paperwork that is used. This includes the client's contact details; date of birth; the referral route, that is, how they found you as a therapist (which not only gives you information about the client's route in finding you, but also provides ongoing data about your own practice marketing), and their occupation (if they have one). You might also ask if the client lives alone or with others; if they have any illnesses that might be useful for the therapist to know about, for example, asthma, or any specific needs, especially in relation to disability or difference (see Chapter 8), and GP details, alongside any relevant medication that the client may be taking. Regarding the latter point, therapists might ask this as a pre-emptive move to assist with potential "risk" situations. Equally, some therapists may deem it unnecessary to collect such details at this point. Decisions around these levels of detail need to be carefully considered by the therapist, so they can adopt and practice ways of working which best suit them. In the eventuality of being faced with a client who is unwilling to provide information, such as GP details, it will be important for the therapist to be mindful of employing ethical, relational best practice, as opposed to static binary thinking. Some of the following reflective questions could be helpful here:

- What is the client's main concern about giving this information?
- Are these details absolute necessary for me at this point, to feel safe, and satisfy that I am practising ethically?

- Do I require the client to comply with my practice boundaries around this? If so, why, and how can this be justified under an ethical lens?
- If I make this a condition of working together, what effect could this have on the client?
- On balance, is it more ethical to stick to my practice boundaries around this, or to listen to what the client needs?
- Have I engaged on this issue, in an open, relational way with the client?
- Have I been able to find a consensus with the client on this issue?
- What decision feels most ethical to proceed with?

As with any ethical dilemma, especially ones which we have not faced before, it would also be good practice to reflect on this, retrospectively. A lot of our learning in private practice comes from experiences we have while "on the job". Such experiences can be an opportune time for development, as well as challenging ourselves to be in regular mindful review of our work and our practice policies. Here are some additional retrospective questions to consider:

- What does my ethical framework say about this? Are there any points that I missed in this exchange that I might consider should this situation arise again?
- Overall, do I feel that I was able to take a balanced view in my ethical decision-making, and that I took into consideration all the relevant factors? If not, what might have been the barriers to this?
- What would be the most productive way to discuss this in supervision? Is there anything further I need from my supervisor?

Using our three-dimension model (see Chapter 1), we can see how in such a scenario there might be conflicts between a therapist's desired way of practising in accordance with carefully considered practice boundaries, the clients own needs and wants, and a wider societal and professional context, which places importance on us safeguarding our clients in the best way possible.

In the same way that there are different approaches to conducting initial sessions/assessments between private practitioners working independently, there will also be different experiences for private practitioners working with third parties. In this case, the assessment may be done by someone else within the organisation. Although there are general pros and cons to this, one ethical challenge is that the private practitioner doesn't get to assess the client themselves, and therefore be able to make an informed decision about who they might feel able, competent, and safe to work with. It can often be assumed that the initial session is only about the client deciding which private practitioner they might wish to work with, and while this is of course important, so, too, is the private practitioner themself, making informed decisions on which clients they can/will work with. This could be based on different elements, including the therapist's own competencies, their own life experience, whether they deem themselves to be the best person for the client, as well as issues such as safety. Although a private practitioner may find saying "no" hard, or may not wish to turn clients away, to do so – where needed – is actually an important component of ethical practice.

Exercise

Try speaking to your supervisor about *how* you might say "no", and what you might consider ethically when framing a conversation around this with a prospective client.

Risk assessment

You will note that risk assessment appears on Daisy's "essential" list. For all the reasons we have already discussed previously (around isolation in private practice, and a lack of scaffolding support from others), thinking about this properly is paramount. Good ethical practice in this setting requires therapists ensuring they are not only aware of the facts around what is needed in this process, and be equipped with the right questions to ask, but also that they look at their own confidence levels around working with risk. It is an area that for very good reason often elicits fear and worry in the therapist. These feelings on their own are not necessarily an issue – so long as space is given in the supervision space to explore and process – but what could become an issue is any unhelpful behavioural response that we have in relation to our emotional process, which might include skirting around addressing and working with risk, head-on. Don't be afraid to ask your supervisor to spend a session or more talking about this, so that you feel prepared for when you are faced with a client who is in an extremely difficult place. Other suggestions for increasing your knowledge and confidence levels when working with risk include specific CPD (Continuous Professional Development) training, consulting relevant literature, and the use of peer spaces for support around practicalities, such as designated paperwork or specific resources (anything aside from talking about actual client work). You might also do well to check out the most recent NICE guidelines, NG225 (NICE, 2022).

Practice management – consistency with your contract

A good example of a piece of documentation that is intrinsically linked to your contract is the "Permission to share information" form. Although we are going to look later in this chapter at handling direct requests from external third parties, let us focus here on some of the active choices a therapist might make, with regards to disclosure. These include those difficult situations that a therapist faces, such as where there is serious risk to the client (or to another person). While confidentiality clauses in the contract will allow a private practitioner to break confidentiality without permission, we feel that the client and therapist discussing in depth together, and where possible, agreeing mutually to do so, is of relational benefit. Furthermore, you may also have something in your contract which states what would happen if your client wanted you to share information with an outside agency. Reasons for these types of requests might range from providing proof that the client is attending therapy to more complex scenarios such as disclosing the content of sessions. Referring in the contract to the need for discussion around either of these tricky choices is paramount, as is the mentioning of the "permission to share information" form. This means that in such cases where it becomes necessary to complete this form, both parties have prior expectations from what has been laid out, in the contract. The form will clearly state the name of the person who will be receiving the information, and specifically for what purpose. You might also include briefly what is being shared (although if writing a letter to somebody, it would be advisable to work with the client transparently on this). And finally ensuring the client signs to explicitly state that they have given permission for the information as described, to be released.

Clinical wills

Therapists, like most human beings, may not relish the idea of engaging in uncomfortable thoughts around having a serious illness, being involved in an accident, or dying, and in fact, often, we like to think that these things will never happen to us. But to be a responsible and ethical private practitioner means planning for these eventualities. Despite clinical wills being mentioned either explicitly or implicitly in most of the UK ethical codes, it has taken private practitioners some years to get up to speed with the importance of this. If that still includes you – don't worry, you won't be the only one. But it is important to act on this, and in fact, it is a relatively easy process.

BACP define a clinical will as follows:

> A Clinical Will is a set of instructions made by a therapist, counsellor or coach for what will happen to their practice in the event that they are no longer able to work due to sudden illness or death. As a minimum, it lays out how clients can be contacted and supported if a practitioner is unable to do so themselves. Additionally, a Clinical Will might also include details of other people or organisations related to a practitioner's business that might need to be notified.
>
> (BACP, 2020)

Rather than thinking of a clinical will as a morbid task, or a complicated bureaucratic exercise, instead tune into the important reasons why it is essential we put this in place *for* our clients. Imagine a client turning up for their session, and you not only not being there but them not hearing for days why, and what had happened. Sometimes it can be easy to think of "harm" in line with the extreme, overt examples – behaviour that we might feel far removed from, but in everyday practice it is much more subtle than this. So, this kind of care towards clients would actually fall under a basic principle in our ethical codes around not bringing harm to clients (NCPS, 2023).

Your clinical executor is the designated person who you appoint to act in the event of an unforeseen incident/set of circumstances. In such cases, they will do the basic practical work, including contacting and informing your clients, but will also, ideally, support your clients, including in potentially coming to terms with an unplanned end to their therapy, as well as thinking about helping them to find a new therapist. For this reason, we may wish to appoint someone who is a trusted colleague. Reflecting on who you might want as your clinical executor is a starting point, before even beginning to draw up the will itself. Reach out to somebody you feel you would trust implicitly. Despite it not being a requirement, it often makes sense for the other person to be a private practitioner too, as they may empathise more with the enormity of this process and be more able to support you in getting this in place.

Although setting up the clinical will itself doesn't have to be taxing, it does require sensitivity and responsibility. As therapists, we need to adhere to our commitments around confidentiality, and make sure the client is aware of the existence of a clinical will, and the way confidentiality would be broken, if needed. The will itself can be thought of by private practitioners as a simple set of instructions to your executor, the details of which can become obvious when you consider your own practice. There are the generic things such as how to give instruction on finding and accessing our client's contact information, being sure to either give clear notes on how to contact each client (and where to find that information in their records). Other questions to consider that will be specific to your practice are, if you keep all your information electronically, how will the executor gain access? Will they need usernames and passwords? And if you hold paper records, does part of the will confirm that you have handed over any relevant keys, that is, to your consulting room and/ or your locked filing system.

Task: Have a go at the first draft of your clinical will. Have a think about what absolute necessities need to be included, as well as what details might be unique to your practice. We've started it off for you …

Dear ….,
On this date (…), you agreed to be my clinical executor in the event of my death, sudden illness or in the event of a serious accident. By clinical executor, I mean the person who takes care of my clients and my practice (including any unfinished administration). The tasks you have agreed to are as follows:

•
•

(Continued …)
Here are some further details which will enable you to carry out these duties:

•
•

Regulated vs unregulated: differences between practitioner psychologists and counsellors/ psychotherapists

Practitioner psychologists are required to register with HCPC in order to be able to use their titles when they practice (i.e., counselling or clinical psychologist). It is a regulated profession, with titles protected by law. Counsellors and psychotherapists on the other hand, have the option to be registered with professional bodies, many of whom hold accredited voluntary registers with the PSA. It is not a regulated profession, meaning they can technically still practice even if not registered with such professional bodies. This means that in serious cases of proved misconduct, HCPC can request that a member stop practising, while BACP, UKCP (The UK Council for Psychotherapy), or NCPS (The National Counselling and Psychotherapy Society) and so on can only remove the therapist from their register. For private practitioners, this also means a practical difference around notes and record-keeping, with HCPC registered practitioners required to keep "full, clear and accurate records" for all their clients (HCPC, 2021), whereas this is only a recommendation for counsellors/psychotherapists. For example, UKCP's code of ethics recommends that its members keep notes which are "appropriate to the modality of therapy being practised" (UKCP, 2019).

Sarah Millward, Ethics Manager at BACP, gives some interesting thoughts here on what a counsellor/psychotherapist might consider with regards to record-keeping: www.bacp.co.uk/news/news-from-bacp/blogs/2023/10-janu ary-notes-and-record-keeping/. We would also add to this information that it be advisable for private practitioners, specifically, to call their insurance company concerning the length of time they keep their client notes for (as there might be stipulations within the therapist's policy). Finally, if a private practitioner is keeping notes it is prudent for all therapists to be aware of the difference between factual notes (or progress notes) and accounts of our "process". Regarding the former, it is good ethical practice to write these notes in as factual way as possible, covering just the content of what was discussed in each respective session. Supervision notes, on the other hand, might be considered more about our own therapeutic approach, process, and self-reflection, and so fall within the domain of our own confidentiality.

More on client notes

The private practitioner may find themselves in a situation where their clinical notes are requested by external parties or authorities. If such a request is supported by a court order, or by the client themselves (in line with GDPR law), the practitioner will be obliged to submit them. However, when such notes are requested by other parties, the situation is more complex, and there is usually no straightforward answer. The therapist therefore should be mindful of not instantly submitting their clinical notes to people who hold authority – even if it is the police – without very careful consideration. This stance is indeed supported by British Psychological Society (BPS), which clearly states that we are not obliged to share notes with the police or a solicitor, and they should form a professional judgement before deciding to do so or not (BPS, n.d.). As it effectively means breaking our client's confidentiality (and risks exposing everything that has been discussed during their course of therapy), it requires deep reflection on what therapeutic reasons we may have for doing so – even if the client is giving permission. A court case might lead to solicitors acting for either party, requesting notes. If our client, with whom we have a duty of care, feels that sharing them with their own solicitor could be of best interest to them, remember they can always request their notes directly from us. If they do so, then it moves from an ethical matter to a legal one, as under GDPR law, the client has every right to request the information being held on them, via a "Subject Access Request" (SAR), which must usually be complied with. Any decisions we may make requires sensitive and thorough consideration, discussion in supervision, consultation with your insurance company, and gentle, empathic conversation with our clients.

---

*Note: For any advice on GDPR, the ICO, can be contacted directly: https://ico.org.uk. They are very user-friendly and provides lots of information for small businesses.

A PSA membership body, in the spotlight

We spoke to Dr Susan Dale, the Ethics Lead at British Association for Counselling and Psychotherapy (BACP), to try and get a glimpse into the kinds of queries and issues which were raised by their members, and members of the public. We thought this would be useful for readers, to help identify any gaps in their learning, based on current real-time data coming through the ethics department, at the largest counselling and psychotherapy body. The Ethics Service is part of the Professional Standards team and their focus is assisting members with ethical queries they encounter in practice: www.bacp.co.uk/events-and-resources/ethics-and-standards/. The BACP Professional Conduct team oversee client complaints. Members of the public who might be thinking about making a complaint, will, in the first instance, make contact with the "Get Help" service (formally "Ask Kathleen"), For more information, see: www.bacp.co.uk/about-us/protecting-the-public/professional-conduct/how-to-complain-about-a-bacp-member/

The data held by BACP gives a general overview concerning their entire membership. While it cannot always differentiate between the variety of settings that therapists work in (such as private practice), it is important to note that when it comes to either more common, recurring themes such as boundaries, record-keeping, contracting, and endings, or more complex queries, reflecting the current era, private practitioners face a greater challenge, due to the nature of lone working, that is, the absence of support from an organisational structure, as already discussed in this book. BACP is currently reviewing the 2018 Ethical Framework, and as we reflected together on the last few years, Susan stated what a tough time it was to be a private practitioner at the moment because "everything's changing so fast". The use of technology forms a big part of this, including the rise in online working. Some of the ethical issues include how clear a member might be on what countries/circumstances their insurance companies would cover them for any work undertaken with international clients, as well as considerations around the ability to properly safeguard a client based outside the UK. This is particularly relevant for those using digital mental health platforms, many of which are not based within the UK, but are offering members international clients. There are also potential issues around data protection, especially in countries such as the USA, where GDPR is outside their remit. Further queries around data protection (GDPR) included concerns such as clients being recorded without their permission by a video doorbell, or issues around unexpected changes in the privacy settings of common therapy platforms (such as Zoom). And other modern AI systems that we are likely to have on our phones, such as "virtual assistant technology", also raised ethical questions around things such as the inadvertent recording and dissemination of client data, as well as risks around the use of AI chatbots, such as a client's data being put into one (even accidentally). Susan stressed that the current lack of regulation in the AI industry certainly raised ethical concerns around confidentiality, in particular. But that she felt it is here to stay, so we need to find a way to embrace new technology, while simultaneously paying attention to the challenges.

We chatted about the importance of engaging with ethics; taking the space to consider ethical dilemmas and challenges that can arise in private practice and Susan advocated for innovative ways to aid therapists in this. "Essentials" were also advised, such as agreeing a clear contract for the work.

Other more general issues raised, which might be of interest to private practitioners, include various ethical considerations concerning the rapid growth of psychedelic therapy, specifically around a lack of clarity on the terminology and descriptors for the work; queries connected to conversion therapy (nb the BACP is a signatory on the Memorandum of understanding, which can be viewed here: www.bacp.co.uk/events-and-resources/ethics-and-standards/mou/); and whether therapists are reflecting enough on EDI (Equality, Diversity and Inclusion) within their practice.

BACP's new ethical framework is due to be published in 2025/2026.

Administration: not just an after-thought

Case Study: Martin has recently started his private practice. He qualified a few months ago as a therapist and is pleased with how he has gone about setting up his practice. He has had one session with a private practice consultant on "growing his practice"; has found a supervisor who works in the sector, has created a website and chosen to join some directories, and has set up a designated business social media Instagram account. All this hard work seems to be paying off for Martin, and his practice grows quickly. However, as time goes on, he's finding it more difficult to keep on top of some of his basic admin. Between his client work, and the "practical task" of growing his practice, which includes daily posts on his social media account, he doesn't seem to have the space or energy to attend to it. Five weeks go by, and he feels overwhelmed and like he is a failure. He tells his supervisor his disappointment at working so hard to control the growth of his practice, but now just feels depleted and despondent.

Many private practitioners will find themselves in a similar position to Martin. As there are so many elements to private practice, it may not be surprising that keeping on top of everything can be challenging. We are all different too, and as discussed in Chapter 2, some of us, as trained therapists, will struggle with aspects of the business side of private practice. As we can see, Martin coped okay with the marketing side of things, but found coping with the administrative load more difficult. It is important that we can leave enough space to tackle every part of private practice, and that we are realistic in the time we set aside for this. Again, returning to difference, we would do well to be caring and respectful to who we are as people. For example, someone who is neurodivergent may find organisation more difficult, and would therefore need to allocate more time to this, as well as potentially drawing on others (such as their supervisor) for support.

TAKE-AWAY MESSAGES: It's our ethical responsibility as private practitioners to pay attention to our practice management. Is it possible to balance, being reflective and diligent, with kindness to ourselves? And in recognition that we are qualified therapists living a "second" career as a businessperson, can we find useful ways to help us commit to this part of our practice, by knowing how we engage with such things, and giving ourselves what we need to maximise our potential?

References

BACP (2020). *Clinical will and digital legacies in the counselling professions.* GPiA 104. BACP. www.bacp.co.uk/events-and-resources/ethics-and-standards/good-practice-in-action/publications/gpia104-clinical-wills-and-digital-legacies-in-the-counselling-professions-fs/

BPS (British Psychological Society) (n.d.). *In a legal setting, who can have access to my therapy notes?* BPS. www.bps.org.uk/faqs/legal-setting-who-can-have-access-my-therapy-notes

HCPC (2021). *Records keeping and the standards.* HCPC. www.hcpc-uk.org/standards/meeting-our-standards/record-keeping/our-expectations-for-your-record-keeping/

NICE (National Institute for health and Care Excellence) (2002). *Self-harm: assessment, management, and preventing recurrence.* NICE guideline [NG225]. www.nice.org.uk/guidance/ng225

NCPS (National Counselling and Psychotherapy Society) (2023). *Code of ethical practice.* NCPS. https://nationalcounsellingsociety.org/assets/uploads/docs/National-Counselling-Society-Code-of-Ethics.pdf

UKCP (The UK Council for Psychotherapy) (2019). *UKCP code of ethics and professional practice.* UKCP. www.psychotherapy.org.uk/media/bkjdm33f/ukcp-code-of-ethics-and-professional-practice-2019.pdf

Chapter 4

Getting yourself seen!

Ethical marketing, in a 21st-century practice

Caz Binstead and Nicholas Sarantakis

Marketing and branding are crucial elements of setting up a private practice. After all, what is the use in developing your practice, and feeling that you have a lot to offer as a therapist, if nobody knows you are there! What we will aim to do in this chapter is to ask how a private practitioner can market their practices, taking into consideration the importance this holds when it comes to growing our businesses, and in a way that upholds best ethical practice. We have already discussed how starting a business is not something that is covered in a lot of trainings, and that for some therapists, they might feel like a fish out of water when it comes to this side of private practice. The marketing side of things is an integral part of the business side of things, and for some therapists, it can feel intimidating to be "out there" on one's own, and even more scary to be showing oneself and feeling comfortable marketing your service; a lot of which is actually just you! It is a big topic, and we are picking out some of the key themes that will hopefully help you find your feet and start to think about the delicate balances between being a business owner and a therapy professional.

Exercise

Think about some of these terms, and jot down what relevance you think they have to a therapy business, and how they might help you market your private practice. If you need to look up the definitions of some of them, don't worry, you won't be alone in that!

- Branding
- Unique selling proposition (USP)
- Search Engine Optimisation (SEO)
- Advertising

DOI: 10.4324/9781003435624-4

- Website
- URL
- Hosting
- Blogging
- Directories
- Google Business
- Copywriting
- Target Market/ideal client base.

What methods of advertising are commonly used

It is a well-known fact that marketing for contemporary private practice is often seen as web-based only. However, in fact, this only makes up one part of therapy marketing. In this book we are referring to *relational ethics*, and it is paramount that this is not forgotten in marketing the type of service we are offering. A lot of therapists would agree that it is the relationship which heals (Yalom, 2000), so if we acknowledge that the relational forms a major part of our work then we need also to acknowledge that this needs to be factored into our marketing. Relationships are made up of the real substance of human beings, who meet and interact. As the work is about the client, we clearly do not bring our full selves, and, rightly, focus on our client's lives only. Yet we will, and do, show parts of our authentic selves, and, in who we are, within our therapeutic relationships. This will come through our exchanges; how we speak; what qualities we embody (such as gentleness, or signs of a high energy personality); how we use humour in the room, and so on. And we also may show the odd glimpse of our personal belief systems, our cultural identity, or how we like to present ourselves, in aspects such as our jewellery. Although the concept of the "blank screen" has long been around in the therapy profession worldwide, in relational therapy it has largely lost its appeal. There will be variation between what therapists choose to show, or not show to their clients. One therapist may choose to wear neutral clothes, perhaps because, personally, they do not want any of themselves imposing on the work, and yet they may still, in the practice of relational therapy, be relaxed and open within their exchanges with the client, showing elements of who they are. Another therapist may choose to wear their wedding ring because they view it as an essential part of who they are, and do not see why they should be expected to take it off for their work, whereas someone else may remove it, seeing that as too much personal information. The point is, that to be relational and authentic, *and* to be ever mindful of our ethical commitments to not encroach on the client's space with our own lives, is not straightforward! So, too, in our marketing, we must be reflective on what elements of ourselves we want to show, understanding how these decisions fit with our philosophy of practice.

Given "marketing" technically concerns the promotion or selling of a counselling and psychotherapy service, we are faced with an interesting challenge. As therapists, we must ensure we are portraying our training and competency honestly, and that we are not in danger of exploiting any potential clients. However, as private practitioners, we are in fact selling a service (whether we like this term of not), which the business side of private practice asks us to lean into. The question therefore must be, how can we do this in an ethical way?

Thistle, in his 1998 book *Counselling and Psychotherapy in Private Practice*, remarks that the BAC (now, the BACP), in their *Code of Ethics and Practice for Counsellors*, stated that the advertising of a private practitioner ought to be limited to: "name, relevant qualifications, telephone number, address, your availability, and a brief listing of services offered" (Thistle, 1998). Time has moved on since then, and yet we observe that most of the ethical codes we looked at (as of summer 2023) focused less on *how* a private practitioner can be fully authentic in their marketing, and more on how a therapist advertising their services must make sure they are being factual in terms of their skills and qualifications. Notwithstanding the importance of such facts when it comes to protecting clients (as well as being an element of representing who the private practitioner is), therapists being able to express a subjective opinion about who they are, and what they can uniquely offer a client, is a real-time actuality that comes with running a therapy business. It is one of the potential conflicts between "the business" and the "therapeutic side", and that needs to not be ignored but thought about and worked with. If a therapist takes the time to really reflect and get to know themselves and their practice well, they are actually in a unique position to present themselves as honestly as they can in all their authenticity. This is also likely to make them better able to understand and respect the types of clients they are trying to attract, and thereby give them the best therapeutic service that they can. It can be argued that reflective self-knowledge will enable a practitioner to be *more in line* with important components of ethical practice, such as the ability to display integrity, trustworthiness, wisdom, respect, sincerity, and humility; some of the named aspirational qualities contained within the BACP Ethical Framework (BACP, 2018). Equally, being true to who you are will also make growing and maintaining an ethical private practice a lot easier.

Who are you? Knowing your niche, and the uniqueness you bring

Exercise

Draw a stick person, and insert arrows from the following body parts, ascertaining what skills and competencies you have, and what you bring uniquely as a person:

Brain: What are my qualifications? How would I best describe my personality, and what aspects of this might I show in the room?

Eyes: How do I see the world? Do I have any life philosophies that might make me the therapist I am?

Heart: What am I passionate about as a therapist? What are my values? And what is my philosophy of practice?

Mouth: Do I speak any languages?

Left hand: Am I trained in BSL sign language, or Makaton?

Right hand: What is it I enjoy doing? Am I creative? Would any other hobbies or skills be of use to me in my client work?

Left foot: Do I have any personal experience that helps me in my work? What is the reason I became a therapist? (nb this wouldn't be something that would necessarily have to be used overtly in your marketing, unless you choose to.)

Right foot: What previous work experience have I got? Do I feel any of this helps me as a therapist?

Whole body: What is my cultural background, and how is this reflected in the way I live my life?

Is there anything else you might add? For instance, when thinking about what makes you unique, don't be afraid to really get into the detail. This case study explores the benefits of being a "night owl":

Case Study: Farah is a private practitioner who works near the City of London. For the whole of her life, she has organically slept until late morning, and stayed up into the early hours before going to bed. When she started her practice (six years ago), she didn't even consider doing daytime work, and naturally gravitated towards working in the evenings. On a couple of days, the latest slot that she offers is at 10 pm. She always has clients who are interested in it, because the location that she works in, coupled with the presenting issues in which she specialises (anxiety, self-worth, and perfectionism), means that she attracts a lot of lawyers and bankers – professions which typically encourage working outside of the 9 am–5 pm pattern. Recently, she has noted some other private practitioners on social media, talking about how therapy should not be conducted at late hours, and that there should be an example being set to clients about "healthy" habits and self-care, including getting up early and not staying up late. Farah does not see her own lifestyle as unhealthy and is aware of the differing views on this subject, particularly around what a person's norm is. She also can see that she is offering a service that many therapists do not offer, which is useful for clients who may not be able to, or wish to, attend earlier in the day. Finally, she recognises from her specialisms and what she has learnt from previous clients, the organisational culture of long working days that operate in many professions. This is an issue that, arguably, needs tackling on a societal level, yet Farah's empathy for clients working in such conditions means she wants to provide a space at times which may increase the likelihood of them engaging with therapy. Despite all this knowledge, she feels shame in front of her contemporaries, and avoids social media conversations on private practice as a result.

Remember that we are all different as people, and whereas there are always wide considerations when it comes to ethical practice, as discussed earlier, if we are honest with ourselves about who we are and what we can offer, this might, in itself, determine what is "ethical" and "unethical". If, on the other hand, Farah had never been a night owl type of person before, she might indeed be risking unethical practice, by being unable to manage working late hours. Such is the importance of personal reflection and self-knowledge. As a community of therapists, it might also be useful to be aware and welcoming of the differences in others and employ a flexible curiosity around how this might affect what constitutes as ethical practice.

Copywriting

Copywriting, or website copy, is crucial when it comes to branding and communicating your USP, that is, your distinct identity, and what you are uniquely offering in your practice. This is not about an expectation of great writing, but more about how wisely you use your words to convey who you are and what you offer, using both implicit and explicit messages. Whenever we talk about something verbally, people will get to know a little more about us, and when a potential client walks into a room, they will get to experience this. So, the importance of roughly who they imagined in their head when they looked at your website or directory listing cannot be understated. If they choose to book an appointment with you based on who they think they can relate to, and on this pivotal notion that we are discussing – that the relationship is a key part of therapy, and there is then a mismatch between what they have read and what they experience upon meeting you – they will be less likely to proceed beyond the initial session. And remember, writing is not just about the content; it's about how the words make someone feel. As humans, we all get a felt sense from the written word, and if as therapists marketing our practices we wish to promote ourselves as a relational practitioner who values authenticity, it is prudent to pay real attention to this. Because by being ourselves (as best as we can), and communicating this in an accurate way via our marketing, it is more likely that we will find what kind of clients best suit us and vice versa. Whether it's talking about our specialisms or encapsulating who we are and thereby portraying how we could best help someone, if your copy can embody the very essence of you, you will be onto a winning strategy in therapy marketing.

One of the authors, Caz, has previously offered a service writing therapists' websites for them and knows all too well how effective this is in private practice marketing. In *Growing your practice – The uniqueness of you* she stresses that this is not necessarily a task that you need to do yourself in order for it to give a real sense of you, and this could be something that a more creative professional writer could do, if it was an investment you felt worth making:

> if writing is not at all your thing, then I would recommend finding a professional writer who will sit with you and listen to you talk about yourself and your practice, so they can infuse a real sense of "you".
>
> (Binstead, 2022)

So be bold with your copywriting, and don't be afraid to let your personality show.

Directories

Your directories are mini versions of your website – windows into the heart of your practice. Optimising all your listings to ensure they are speaking to your ideal client is key to ethical marketing. You may not be able to fit everything from your website into a directory listing, or it might require you moving things around, but remember, as John Kabat-Zinn (2004) says, "wherever you go, there you are"! If we are authentic, and connected to our being as a living, breathing unique person, then we carry our footprint everywhere we go. And so, consistency is not only displaying ethical practice by being honest in who you are and what you offer, it also creates a brand that spans across all profiles and is intricately woven into all elements of your practice design. This includes our chosen profile photo. We need to be mindful of both conveying who we are, but also staying within the realms of good ethical practice. Has anyone read in a Facebook group how a smiley photo is good to have, as people will be more attracted to that?! While the photo does play an important role in how clients choose their therapist, there are other considerations. What if smiling doesn't suit your personality? What about if you choose the most smiley photo, and it was clearly visible that you were at a party? What if your most smiley photo is 15 years old? When choosing a photo, we need to take into consideration our roles as therapists, and the balancing act we are trying to strike within our marketing – being as authentic as we can, without bringing our profession into disrepute, or imposing our lives on potential clients. As authors, we question how the notion of "professionalism" could potentially be used to quash a therapist's identity, by the enforcement of strict rules around how therapist should "be". If we reclaim that word, what we are left with is being proud to be a professional that makes a choice to be committed, ethical, and dedicated to the seriousness of our work as therapists. Someone who is more focused on showing respect to our clients than feeling that we need to subscribe to being a one-size-fits-all approach.

Exercise

Use the reflections above and have a go at writing a directory listing.

Tips:

- Avoid being woolly or non-committal, and instead home in, and give direct, clear, and specific information about who you are and what you offer.
- Be wary of generalisations and over-promising. Rather than ticking every box of things that you work with, see if you can stick to your niche, and show clients what it is that makes you special in what you do.

Building your networks – the art of being seen

By SEO, we mean the best ways to optimise visibility, and this will often involve ways to direct people to your website. It is something that can be paid for, but for therapists, many who have relatively small businesses, finding more cost-effective and steady strategies can be a good option. There are in fact many free ways to build your presence, and a straightforward way to think of it is: "how can I best get Google to like me?!". A good way to achieve this is by your name and business listing appearing in different places on the worldwide web, which Google will detect. If you sign up to free listings, for example – even if you don't think that you'll get many direct referrals – you might still be ticking an important box in terms of building your visibility. One of the more useful free listings is the invaluable Google Business Profile, where you can create a free profile, and add posts or photos, as well as being given a presence on Google maps. There are also ways we can encourage Google to display us in relevant searches by letting it know what our website (and business) is about, such as the use of key words in the content we produce, like blogs (Travis, 2019). Improving visibility on the web is all about improving your Google ranking. To keep an eye on your ranking, you can try putting into the Google search bar some key words that you think a customer would put in to search for what they were looking for. This might be something like "Counselling Oxford Street".

We will also here mention the old-fashioned method of leaflets and business cards. How much these achieve in terms of direct contact with clients might be debatable, and success might be dependent on the area in which you live, that is, if it is a place with a strong emphasis on community, it will be more likely there will be community boards for such things. And this might not just be rural communities – in fact, since the pandemic, it has been notable how in some urban areas such as particular boroughs within London, there has been a rise in appreciation and celebration of community and support for small businesses. Another option is distributing these to other professionals, such as GPs in the area. This might be dependent on the practice manager being open to such offers (and logistics, such as whether the surgery outsources duties around marketing local practices), as well as whether any GPs have expressed an interest in receiving data about local therapists.

Last, but certainly not least, is consideration of the local therapist community. Do you know the other therapists in your area? Sometimes we get stuck on the idea that other professionals in our local community are our competition. The reality is, though, there are enough clients to go around, particularly when we take into consideration the mental health crisis here in the UK (and many other parts of the world), which means lots of clients looking for therapists. If we believe in the premise that different therapists suit different clients, then why not mutually support, and appreciate, each other's uniqueness?! These kind of informal referral circles are different to our therapist friends, or those who work within some kind of group practice. They are consistent, purposeful relationships with other local therapists that take time to build and are based on trust and transparency about who we are, what we stand for, and how we practice. This is a smart way to build practice because it helps create real relationships, which in turn reduces isolation, provides mutual encouragement and reciprocity (instead of the harshness of competitiveness), and helps therapists to grow their practices. It also cements our ethical commitments in practice, by normalising referring someone on when they present something outside of our competency level, or when we just know a client would be better suited elsewhere.

A closer look at ethics in marketing

Case study: Kerry has been working in private practice for 15 years. She would describe herself as a humble person, and her website copywriting is infused with a sense of this. She has recently been discussing with her supervisor putting her fees up, and how she feels she needs to also update her website to better reflect the practitioner she is now. She is someone who has done a lot during her time as a therapist – teaching; supervising; writing articles; contributing to the media, and being active in her profession. She begins to write up some of this, and immediately hits a wall. She thinks about the type of clients she normally attracts, and wonders if they might be put off her list of achievements.

She works a lot with low self-esteem because she has historic personal experience of this, and she doesn't want to risk making potential clients feel worse about themselves than they already might. She is also aware that she looks young, and wonders if by showing explicitly that she had worked for so many years in the profession, it might affect the client base she normally attracts, which are young professionals in their twenties and thirties. She wants to be authentic and best portray the therapist that she is now, but also wants to be able to do it in a way which shows her personal qualities, and that in reality she cares more about relational work than accolades.

Analysis: This is an interesting vignette, and brings up a few questions:

- How can we, in our marketing, balance who we are with what we do?
- Can we always control how the client may view us, and what judgements they may make, and how this sits with how we view ourselves?
- Kerry has already revealed that she herself suffered with low self-esteem. Is Kerry naturally humble in character, or is she still lacking in confidence, and so veering away from assertively stating her achievements? (This question comes with no judgement – it could be one or the other ... the important thing is that the question is asked.)
- Can she continue to work with the same client group, or does she need to review that? Especially given she is planning on putting her fees up, which might also influence what types of clients she attracts.
- She cannot change how young she looks, nor should she have to! But is her photo 15 years old too? If so, that is something she can change, and she would do well to update it, because everybody changes even a little, in that amount of time.
- Can she potentially get some help with her copywriting, to feel more confident in communicating her valuable years of experience, while keeping the relational element alive. A good copy would be able to consider the issues she works with, and how a potential client may feel reading something.

Testimonials

In an age of reviews and recommendations, potential clients may want to seek out testimonials about our practices, like they might for any other business.

But ethically speaking, across the world, they are controversial within our profession. The EAP (European Association for Psychotherapy), the APA (American Psychological Association), and the UKCP have all stated in their ethical codes that testimonials are not allowed in a private practitioner's advertising (APA, 2023; EAP, 2018; UKCP, 2019). Although, the UK's largest membership body, BACP, has not, to date, given an opinion on it. A private practitioner may argue that it is one way a client can get a real feel for how they practice as a therapist, and that they run a business the same as any other, and providing they do not force or put any pressure on clients writing reviews for them, they are entitled to do so. Some therapists may even argue that some of their clients have asked them if they can write a testimonial. Finally, it could be said that as therapy in general is less about "word of mouth" these days (a historic way of gaining clients in our profession), this is a modern-day equivalent. These are, in theory, valid points. However, the ethical considerations that can't be ignored are as follows:

- Do potential clients really get an accurate picture, if therapists only share (or ask for) testimonials from people who think they are good?
- We need to protect our client's confidentiality, and so it is ethically questionable to put a name on a review, although this conflicts with advertising trading standards recommendations.
- Are we respecting a client's autonomy by putting them on the spot and asking for a testimonial (BACP, 2018)?
- Are we being mindful of power dynamics? If we have asked a client to write a testimonial, which they either felt coerced to do (because they were already uncomfortable in the space), or were happy to do at the time, but then realised retrospectively that they were unhappy with the therapy, this could be problematic. As much as we may want them to, the reality is that our clients may not always tell us exactly how they feel. They might appear happy with the therapeutic relationship, and even keep coming every week, but that doesn't necessarily mean that it's true, and we need to be sensitive to this.

The authors wondered whether clients who wish to, through their own autonomy (and if happy to waver their own anonymity), could instead write a review on a therapist's Google listing. Another way of utilising this free service and gaining a boost through a reliable and honest process is to ask any colleagues who know you and your practice well, to write a professional review.

"Topping up"

In this digital age, a way in which a private practitioner can supplement their earnings as a private practitioner is via large digital online therapy platforms. Many of these advertise for therapists, and at a first glance the guaranteed client work can seem like a great solution to the uncertainty of private practice. Although many therapists sign up to these platforms, there are potentially several ethical considerations, some of which were picked up in our interview with Susan from BACP (Chapter 3). All providers will be run in different ways, and here's a fictional case study to ponder on:

> **Case Study**: Will joined a growing online therapy platform a year and a half into his private practice. At first, he was optimistic, and to supplement his income he took a lot of weight off his shoulders. He joined a help group aligned with the platform and enjoyed networking with other therapists working there. However, within a few months, Will began to feel more and more tired. He was agreeing to take on lots of clients from the platform, and yet because the company's client cancellation policy was a very short amount of time, he found that often the sessions would be cancelled at short notice. He was stuck in a cycle of taking on more clients to try to regain money lost from cancelled clients, only to be met with more cancellations. He found that he was spending a lot of time and effort on work that didn't transpire – time that could have, instead, gone on his own private practice. He found it so psychologically and physically exhausting that it no longer felt to him like just "top-up" work, secondary to his private practice.

Qualifications, accreditations, registrations, and regulation

The listing of qualifications and registrations on a private practitioner's website is a practice that is commonplace in the UK. The authors recognise and endorse the view that the public should be protected from individuals in private practice, who claim to be therapists but do not have adequate training. We noted that some formal ethical codes that we looked at, beyond the UK (APA, 2023; EAP, 2018), suggest that a private practitioner should be allowed to advertise their services as long as their training is accredited by the regional (in the USA), or national, professional body. However, sometimes practitioners have an alternative type of training, which might still be satisfactory for working with clients, but is not accredited by one of the major professional bodies, simply because it is underpinned by a different therapeutic philosophy. This therefore becomes tricky and raises questions about major professional bodies being granted sole power in deciding who can legitimately practice or not. In the UK, the authors equally believe that practitioners should have the right to use the professional qualifications and/or titles that have been granted by their training institutes, regardless of whether they are registered with a *particular* professional body. For example, a Counselling or Clinical Psychologist who obtained their doctorate from a properly accredited training programme may choose not to join HCPC (which currently has the monopoly of regulating "protected titles"), instead aligning with another professional body, such as The Independent Practitioners Network. They may do this because they legitimately feel this body is closer to their professional values. The authors wondered about there being space to consider an underlying principle of believing that such fully qualified practitioners are themselves, capable of holding a degree of self-autonomy where they commit to being transparent about their training, their principles of practice, and the basis of their work with clients, and take responsibility for this, in the advertising of their practice.

What might this look like in action?

In respecting the rich diversity of our profession, this might look different for different therapists. Some may choose to make explicit reference to the accreditation of their training by a professional body, and state that they apply specific research-evidenced models (such as Cognitive Behavioural Therapy). While other practitioners may share publicly that they completed a type of training that is more relational, and that they may not be regulated, accredited, or registered by one of the major professional bodies. There are independent bodies that exist, which carry their own complaints procedures (allowing the client to complain, if needed) and ethical guidelines, and therefore uphold the principles of ethical practice that we all, as qualified therapists, ought to be committing to. It's also worth noting that even private practitioners who are not aligned with a major membership body can still choose to subscribe to whichever ethical code they feel makes most sense to them as a practitioner. BACP Ethical Framework, for example, is open to the public, and therefore not just restricted for use by their members. The authors feel it important that private practitioners align with membership associations which adequately represent the values they hold themselves, around best practice and accountability. Being clear that you are not communicating deceptive or false information, and being transparent in your marketing about your training, registrations/memberships, and the background and basis of your practice (including, displaying which ethical framework you adhere to), is key. These kinds of principles matter even more nowadays, given that the pluralistic nature of the counselling and psychotherapy world, and of society as a whole, is more recognised. We believe our profession should reflect the very diverse needs and preferences of our clientele.

TAKE-AWAY MESSAGES: There are many different considerations when it comes to marketing a private practice, so giving real thought around what might work best for your individual business is vital. Remember that being confident that you are engaging with ethical marketing will help embolden you to embrace the uniqueness that you bring within your practice.

References

APA (2023). *Ethical principles of psychologists and code of conduct*. APA. www.apa. org/ethics/code

BACP (2018). *Ethical framework for the counselling professions*. BACP. www. bacp.co.uk/media/3103/bacp-ethical-framework-for-the-counselling-professions-2018.pdf

Binstead, C. (2022). *Growing your practice: the uniqueness of you*. BACP. www. bacp.co.uk/bacp-divisions/bacp-private-practice/private-practice-toolkit/growing-your-practice-the-uniqueness-of-you/

EAP (European Association for Psychotherapy) (2018). *EAP statement of ethical principles*. EAP. www.europsyche.org/quality-standards/eap-guidelines/statement-of-ethical-principles/

Kabat-Zinn, J. (2004). *Wherever you go, there you are*. Piatkus.

Thistle, R. (1998). *Counselling and psychotherapy in private practice*. SAGE.

Travis, J. (2019). *Grow your private practice*. Self published.

UKCP (2019). *UKCP code of ethics and professional practice*. UKCP. www.psycho
therapy.org.uk/media/bkjdm33f/ukcp-code-of-ethics-and-professional-practice-
2019.pdf
Yalom, I. D. (2000). *Love's executioner*. Harper Perennial Modern.

Chapter 5

Building your practice

Contracting and engagement

Caz Binstead and Nicholas Sarantakis

One of the most important things for a private practitioner to consider is their contract. Our general engagements with a client from the very first session, and the agreements we build via a contract, verbal or written (we look at the difference between the two later), is of utmost importance. Why? Because this is when we begin to partake in a relational exchange with the client, which encompasses both the start of a potential working alliance (Clarkson, 2003) and a business relationship. It is the time that we explain how our practice works, and let the client know about our individual business boundaries (Travis & Binstead, 2022), as well as beginning to communicate our therapeutic boundaries (Williams, 2023). And, being aware of the thin line between these.

The initial contact point that we have with clients also forms the start of you as a private practitioner, setting out how you run your individual practice, and communicating this clearly through words and actions to prospective clients.

Both of these are crucial elements which make up how a private practitioner is building a solid frame for clients (and themselves), in order to safely practice therapy. Consistent, clear boundaries is the fairness we give to clients, and embody important elements of our commitments to ethical practice, such as an assurance to not cause them harm. It is about respecting clients and putting them first, by providing information about therapy and your practice, that is transparent and not likely to lead to confusion. It also in turn helps you, the private practitioner, because it gives you a chance to really think about what boundaries you want in place for your business. This may be a developing process as you move along, and don't be afraid to re-consider points on your original contract, if you find that things you originally thought would work, do not (with any new clients coming through, only). The reason why this is an important individualised exercise is because

DOI: 10.4324/9781003435624-5

we need to feel okay with what we decide. Of course, like other elements of private practice, there are bits of collective knowledge, and some absolute ethical "musts" for the contract, but some of the finer details will be things that: i) is reasonable for clients, and (in your judgement) is bringing ethical fair practice, and ii) you know works solely for you, and your practice. The last thing you want is to copy someone else's contract word for word, without considering how workable it might be for you. And this is crucial, because a private practitioner who doesn't feel comfortable with their contract is likely to have shaky, inconsistent boundaries, which can lead to some of the biggest issues within the private practice setting. Have a think about the importance of boundaries in any relationship – implementing boundaries is something that as therapists, we are likely to remind our clients of, particularly when it comes to attempting to feel safe in a relationship. Now throw in the power we have as therapists and consider how easy it might be for us to inadvertently harm clients through something like a lack of clarity. Let's go even deeper, and consider the role of money, and how handling money in private practice has a direct effect on power dynamics, whether we like it or not. So, on both a relational and business level, having a contract that reflects a realistic and fair set of understandings between you both and thinking about how this is delivered at the start of the work is very important. Some people call the contract an "agreement" instead, which emphasises the relational element. This word seems to overtly emphasise the importance of the mutual experience, especially around expectations that both parties have going forward.

Before we look more closely at initial engagement with clients, and contracting, from a practical stance, here's a few more theoretical recommendations for adherence to ethical practice:

- Be clear with clients in the **initial engagement** what the various stages are from the point of them having contacted you, to meeting for the first time in-person. This is going to look different for each private practitioner, and so clients need gentle but direct guidance. They will also, in the first instance, need any information around your practice boundaries, that might dictate whether you are going to be the right therapist for them. An example of this might be communicating if you have set slots for clients (nor not), as some people may not be able to attend the same time each week and would therefore need to know this straight away.
- Communicating and explaining how you operate **initial sessions**. As private practitioners have differing ways regarding the first session, in terms

of the mode of delivery, whether it's free or not, whether it's a full-length session, it's good to communicate this in the first instance. There's a case study looking at this later in the chapter.

- Consider a **written contract**, as opposed to a verbal one. It's not an ethical requirement, but one of the authors (Caz) states this to be her number one top tip, for protecting clients as well as yourself. This is connected to the point already made about clarity. If something is verbal, there is more chance that a client might forget what has been said or misunderstand something. On the client's side, such confusions can cause distress or hurt. If it leads to a dispute, this can sometimes then lead to complaints being made. For circumstances where this goes to a professional conduct panel or licensing board, a private practitioner needs to be aware that not having your agreement in written form means you can't show the actual parameters of the work, and therefore makes it much harder to defend yourself.
- Consider getting the client to **sign the contract** or, **state in written form (such as on an email, if working online) that they agree**. This is good practice in terms of formalising those joint expectations of the space, and forthcoming sessions.
- **Talk through** the written contract with the client. If we agree that ethics are relational, then chatting through and opening up the space for clients to ask any questions allows the words on the page to come alive. It is also a good ethical move, in terms of maintaining your practice (which in business terms here means having a caseload of clients). If as a private practitioner you send the contract by email only, and never refer to it with the client, it potentially leaves you open to relational problems down the line. For example, if a client isn't 100% happy with every aspect of your contractual practice boundaries, ideally that would be talked about, to see if proceeding with you is the right thing for them. But remember, not every client will initiate such conversations, especially via email, so without a designated space and time, unspoken information may get lost, meaning those kinds of considerations would not be possible. Getting off on the right footing, by allowing space for the client to express what they need to, is a great example of relational ethics at work. If a client isn't happy though, this doesn't mean we have to re-negotiate our contracts. Sometimes, it's about just respecting the client's feelings, and reminding them that another therapist's practice boundaries may suit them better. It's much better for the private practitioner to work with the clients that are right for them (and vice versa),

rather than trying to "convert" every enquiry into a client. That last sentence is an example of a "taboo" subject (as previously mentioned) that we are bringing to the surface. One of the many potential conflict areas in private practice between the business side and the ethical therapeutic practice.

- A recommendation would be to draw up the contract yourself, and then take it along for **discussion in supervision**. Remember what we said in Chapter 2 about how it's much easier in an organisational setting, because someone else has likely drawn up the contract. Getting an outside opinion is a good idea, and who better than your supervisor, who is central to your development as a private practitioner.

- **Commit** to what you put in your contract. This doesn't mean it needs to be set in stone, and it can change, but for each client that you contract with it's important to recognise you are making a commitment, just as much as them. This commitment will also allow time, to see if what you have put in place works or if you wish to update/refresh any parts of your contract as you develop your practice. Commitment also allows us to recognise more clearly when we are choosing to apply conscious flexibility (see point below).

- Remember that for therapeutic reasons we may well **bend an original boundary** *on the odd occasion*. This would be when we feel it would be beneficial for the work, or the client. Boundaries can be comparable to a bamboo tree that flexes when the wind blows; neither breaking nor staying rigid. Our boundaries are not "rules", but terms that are in place so that all parties are aware of the parameters in which you generally operate. When you do decide to bend a boundary, it's important that you make what you are doing very clear to the client, to avoid any confusion (particularly in the future). It's also important, especially in private practice, that we are doing so, for the benefit of the work or the client – not to make our lives easier, or because we find applying a boundary difficult. In this chapter, we've included a case study on this point.

- In certain instances, we can also **re-negotiate the original contract** signed with a client. This requires careful thought, and, ideally, discussion in supervision. One of the instances might be if you need to make a change – say, you're moving therapy space, and so you require meeting in a different venue. A more complex one might be an extension of that: you're moving therapy space and the new venue doesn't have the same availability, therefore you need to ask the client to re-negotiate the time that you meet. You'll note that I have written "ask" because essentially that's what re-negotiation is about. You essentially need them to affirm any changes you're making, to be able to re-negotiate and agree mutually that you are continuing the work under these new terms. Another example might be where you make the choice to re-negotiate a point in your contact, based on what feels best for a *particular* client. Again, this is not a decision that should be taken lightly, and in the context of private practice it's useful to think about any implications any changes might mean for you too, especially as a business owner.

- Consider in your contract your **philosophy of therapy**, as well as **your business**. There is a case study in this chapter on whether a therapist might offer fortnightly sessions (or not), and how that concerns the former, the latter, or both.
- Don't be afraid to **return** to your contract with your client, during the work, if you feel it would be beneficial for the client, the work, and/or the therapeutic relationship.
- Concerning more **generic** parts of the contract, be up-to-date with what might be included for ethical reasons, e.g. cancellation policy; what might be included for legal reasons, e.g. GDPR, and what might cover both, e.g confidentiality clause.
- When we consider the **individualised** aspects of our contract, as well as any needs and wants that you have for you and your business, think also about any individualised specific practicalities. As discussed in a case study in Chapter 1, an example of this might be that if you live and work in the same place, you ensure that you discuss with the client how you manage eventualities such as bumping into each other.
- It's good to try and **endeavour** to be reasonable and fair, but remember that these words can be subjective, i.e., what seems fair to you may not seem fair to a client. So long as you are not putting something in your business boundaries which is extremely unreasonable and could constitute as harm to the client, then the most important aspect is how you, yourself, feel about them. This doesn't only serve your needs, but will also make it easier to commit to on a consistent basis.
- Keep these words at the heart of contract making: **consistent, detailed, clear, realistic and workable**, and **curated with the intention of 'doing no harm' to the client**.

Initial contact – three case studies

Case Study: Juniper has read in a magazine that it is advisable to contact several therapists to arrange an initial session, to find the "right fit". She has taken her time researching people in her local area, and has created a list of private practitioners that she thinks potentially sound right for her. The first two meetings that she arranges are full 50-minute sessions in-person, which she has been informed are chargeable (at the same rate as all other sessions). The third therapist that she has contacted, Bill, responds to her enquiry offering her a 30-minute "chat", but does not stipulate how this would take place, or whether it is chargeable. Juniper feels confused at the difference – she assumes it might be free as it is shorter but feels embarrassed to ask. She also wonders if she can properly ascertain what she needs to from a shorter session, and is worried about feeling pressured to "sign up" to something prematurely.

Let's look at this example theoretically, through the three-dimensional model:

Client: Juniper is taking the business of finding a therapist seriously. For us who work in this sector, it can sometimes be easy to forget what a big deal starting therapy can be for clients. Juniper is trying her best to do it in a systematic way, but she becomes anxious when there is a curveball. The issue here is not so much Bill's offering, but more about the lack of clarity. Juniper, as a potential client, deserves to be met with guidance which helps her navigate with ease her route into therapy.

Therapist: First off, we know as much information as Juniper, but let's suppose that the session is indeed free. Bill might think that he is helping clients out in this. Many clients, afterall, do look for free initial sessions. But in Juniper's case, she is willing to pay. As a customer (marketing speak), he has lost touch with her needs at the first instance, and as a therapy client, he has clearly caused her inadvertent discomfort. Bear in mind, we don't know yet why she is coming to therapy (it could be for anxiety-related reasons).

Societal: It's useful for our sector to work symbiotically with outlets such as the media, in presenting therapy in contemporary times as more of a normalised thing. Inaccessibility to free therapy can be an issue, so when people approach a private practitioner, it's important that they come across as professional and robust, thereby easing the process for the prospective client.

Conclusion: Bill might lose Juniper automatically as a potential client if she feels put off by this first exchange. In which case, this situation has failed to benefit either of them. Going forward Bill would do well to be more detailed in his response to clients, providing them with all the information they need in the first instance. If his first session is free, this is certainly going to suit some clients, and be of benefit. It's also worth remembering that some private practitioners will do a hybrid version of what we might refer to as first discussions. For instance, you may offer a short phone-call, say 10 minutes, to go over practicalities with a potential client, and to just check if, theoretically, you could work with them, e.g. that they are within your competency levels etc., before proceeding with an official initial (paid) session.

Case Study: Niall only offers weekly sessions. A potential client, Sam, asks if they can meet fortnightly, so Niall replies stating that unfortunately he doesn't offer this, giving his reasons. Later on, he discusses this in a peer supervision group, and a group member reprimands him, and tells him that he indeed "should" offer fortnightly, because not doing so might not be respecting what a client wants.

Exercise

Discuss this example in your own supervision space. Consider the following:

- What reasons, in line with a particular modality/philosophy of therapy, might be given by a therapist for not offering fortnightly sessions?
- What reasons, in line with chosen business boundaries, might be given by a therapist for not offering fortnightly sessions?
- How might a therapist like Niall communicate any of these reasons in a way that respects the client's feelings?
- What further guidance could be given?
- What do you think about the peer supervisee's view?
- How can Niall communicate his boundaries around this contractually, and how might he reflect on/prepare for managing the possibility of any existing clients wanting to move to fortnightly later down the line?

> **Case Study**: Lily has contacted lots of private practitioners and has had quite a low response rate. She tells her friend, Vicky, who happens to be a trained counsellor, and feeling upset about it, Vicky posts in a Facebook group about how awful it is for a private practitioner to not respond to an enquiry. There are lots of "likes", and comments agreeing, calling such therapists "unethical". Judy sees the post, and instantly feels ashamed, because she knows that there are a few enquiries from the past two weeks which she has yet to respond to. She is aware that she has been dealing with some difficulties in her personal life and is tired, so is finding it harder to keep on top of her administration. Despite this, she feels like a bad therapist now, and that she must be unethical.

Analysis: Let's look at this one using our three-dimensional model:

Client: There needs to be huge empathy for Lily, and any client who feels that they have been left waiting for a response. Returning to our earlier point about how big a big deal it is to look for a therapist, it must feel understandably difficult when you do not hear back from a number of those you have contacted. It is a therapist's responsibility to be mindful about how easy it might be for a potential client to feel hurt, rejected, powerless, and so on, by a lack of response.

Therapist: Private practitioners like Judy, do get overwhelmed at times. It's part of being human, and a toll of the amount we carry as therapists. Sometimes, even when it "should" be possible, the ability to keep on top of everything, in fact, might be a challenge. And when such times arise, a therapist's focus and energy will likely be reserved for their existing clients. It doesn't make not responding to enquires right, but it does provide an explanation.

Society: All therapists need to be aware of not undermining public confidence (NCPS, 2023), and responding to clients, and not causing further distress, would clearly be part of this. On a community societal level, while it is clearly good to have conversations, which bring a spotlight on issues in our profession, in the example given, we can see the effect it has on Judy. There is something about this post, with its thread of comments, that has left her feeling shamed. Given some of her thoughts, we might wonder about the impact on her confidence levels as a therapist. We might also wonder whether this will increase the likelihood of her discussing her management of this in supervision (which would be most useful), or decrease it?

Conclusion: It is ideal to respond to all client enquiries as soon as you can. But as human beings too, there might be restrictions to this at times, or "blips". Another thing to consider is the pieces of information we don't know from the example, such as when Lily contacted these therapists, and what her own expectations are in terms of how quickly she might get a reply. Private practitioners are going to have different expectations around this too. There might be an argument to say that if you have a very difficult or tiring week, it might make better sense (for both therapist and client) to wait a few days to respond, until you feel in a better mind-frame. Remember, there is a difference between someone not responding for a week, and someone not responding at all. It would be good for Judy to reflect on her own experiences; both around her current difficulties in managing enquires, and on how she makes sense of this feeling of shame that has arisen within her. A practical thing she could do in the meantime is put on her email auto-response to advise clients that she is not attending to emails, which perhaps includes some general recommendations for people (such as directory listings). Although, of course, there are therapists unfortunately who do not reflect enough on ethics, it's worth the community of private practitioners remembering that we are unlikely to learn from being shamed; that this is not always an easy sector to work in, and that surely we all at times have our own developmental points to work on.

Aspects of the contract

*Please note, the following aims to give a general idea about what might be included in a contract, and is not an exhaustive list.

Any contract should include basic details such as your name, contact details, and who you are registered or accredited with/regulated by. It will be clear that the contract is between you and the client, and may include what day/time you and the client will meet (if the same each week). It needs to say how long sessions are, and by what mode/in what location these will be conducted. You will also likely put some general information about your practice, such as how you work (although hopefully a client will have been able to have read your website or directories in advance), your supervision arrangements, if you are meeting clients on a weekly/fortnightly basis and how clients can pay you. All private practice contracts ought to include a section on cancellations and holidays, which gives us much detail as possible, including your definition of these terms. And, it's good to also have a note about what your practice boundaries are around a client being late. Similarly, there needs to be a section on confidentiality, which will cover every facet of potentially breaking confidentiality. And GDPR can either be mentioned in the contract or in a separate privacy notice. You may wish to say something about expectations around the length of work, that is, if you offer short term, long term (open-ended), or both; if you have any specific stipulations (including, if you offer weekly/fortnightly etc.), or if you have set review points, for example, at the six-point mark.

If you want further guidance, and are a BACP member, one of the author's (Caz) co-wrote a contract template (with David Lloyd-Brown) which you might want to check out for guidance (free resource) – www.bacp.co.uk/media/16012/bacp-pp-toolkit-contract-discussions-private-practitioners-contracting-template.pdf). Alternatively, *Setting Up and Running a Therapy Business* by James Rye includes some useful thoughts (*note: this book was published in 2017, so some of the information might be dated).

For the rest of this chapter, we are homing in on the ethics around some specific areas of contracting and practice boundaries. If you're setting up your own contract, see if you can use the guidance in this chapter and beyond, and then focus on researching further, and, through creativity and deep reflection, begin to build your own practice contract. Poonam is just at the beginning of this process.

Poonam's list of questions to reflect on:

- What are the things in which I am legally required to break confidentiality?
- I want to have set slots, because I think it suits me better, but I'm worried I'll miss out on clients because of that. What's my priority – growing my practice in the short term or putting in place practice boundaries which suit me? My task is to do a pros and cons list and discuss this in supervision.
- I'm very unsure about setting a cancellation policy. How on earth am I going to decide?! I have noted that I don't have to keep what I choose forever, so this takes the pressure off a bit. Maybe I need to discuss in supervision and with peers, and then just try and make a decision that feels right for me.

- I wonder what happens if I'm working with someone with an alcohol dependency. What if they turn up to the session drunk? I think this needs to be addressed in some way in the contract, and, perhaps, relationally with the client too.
- I use social media a lot. Does this need to be in my contract? I'm not sure … I think this is something I need to reflect more on.

Practice boundaries – contact between sessions

The levels of contact that you have with a client in-between sessions is not set in stone, and may concern not just how you wish to run your private practice (and the boundaries you wish to put in place to reflect that), but also how you practice therapeutically. Whatever choices you make, though, a level of consistency and clarity with this is essential, so that mutual expectations within the work are laid out and understood in the same way by each party. "Contact in-between" generally refers to a few different definitions, which will probably require their own specific descriptions:

1. General contact: In the age of email, it has become far more common for clients to expect that they can contact their therapist at any time, giving practical information or requests. An example of this might be that the client wishes to book off a holiday day and might feel they are being efficient by emailing this information in advance. For some therapists, this is going to be okay with them. But there are considerations you may wish to take into account, especially around how much you are in "work-mode" outside of clients. If you have a smaller practice, this may feel more manageable, but if you are seeing 20 clients a week, and all of them emailed over a period of two days to give you some information, you may very quickly feel overwhelmed. Especially, when managing this with other administrative aspects of your practice, such as incoming enquiries. If you do decide to allow your emails to be constantly open in this way, it might be useful to put your own boundaries around this, such as times of the day/week in which you deal with such emails. And this of course can be communicated to the client in the contract too, to make them aware if, for instance, they will/ will not get an instant response. On the other hand, you may decide instead to put a pause on any non-urgent (email or other) communication, during the work. This can be said in a clear and direct way such as: "once we start working together, all email communication will cease" (with reference to

other points, such as how they might contact you in an emergency). Even if this appears to you as harsh or not in line with what might be considered "normal" social interaction today, it is better to be upfront about this from the outset if you would rather not manage it. It would also be fair to refer in another point in the contract, how the client can instead bring something to your attention should they wish to. It could be argued that putting in such boundaries can also provide a good opportunity, to model to clients that although the work is relational, it is a professional relationship, and different to that of a friendship.

2. Emergency contact: This type of contact is obviously different, and we have an ethical obligation as therapists to respond to our clients appropriately, should they find themselves in an emergency. It's important that we consider what form of communication is going to realistically suit us best. For example, if you have a separate work phone, but you don't look at it too often throughout the day, and maybe sometimes leave it at home, this could be very problematic if a client tried to contact you in an emergency. So be mindful to let your clients know in your contract what method works best. It can work well having this information on a different point to the one above, because it shows that you are separating them out in your mind, thereby communicating to your client in an unspoken way your understanding of the difference between an emergency situation, and something that does not need quick attention, and could wait until the next session.

    Note: Even with messages that require more urgent action, you may wish to give some kind of indication as to when you will be able to reply to messages. Even for absolute emergencies, the likelihood is that we may not be available at a time such as 3 am. Putting some timings around when you consider your practice, and your work phone or emails to be "open", is useful and realistic information for clients.

3. There is another reason for contact that perhaps sits between the "general" and the "emergency" camp, and these are messages from clients that i) need to be sent (and seen by the therapist), and ii) due to their nature, come with short notice. Two examples of this might be, first, that the client is sick and needs to cancel the session, and second, that the client is running late for the session, and wishes to inform their therapist. Depending on the unique decisions you have made for your practice in points 1 and 2, you may incorporate this into whichever seems the most relevant.

4. The last type of communication is that which is more therapeutic. It might not be an absolute emergency (technically speaking), but for whatever reason, the client may wish to seek contact with you, or send you something that is directly linked to the work you are doing. This may be a situation where it could be important to consider whether you will flex your boundaries, depending on what is happening in the work, and what you think could be therapeutically beneficial. Be sure to talk with your supervisor if you can, and if not, reflect and tune into your client, and what you feel might be happening. Perhaps, therapeutically, they need a response from you – even if it's not something you would normally do. How much you engage will be up to you, and how you choose to manage this will be integral to your therapy work and your relationship with your client. But the most important thing is to not muddy the waters between the business and the therapy, even if they overlap. It's not an invitation to start breaking any of your business boundaries with no proper reason or benefit, but to bend a boundary and have an understanding why you are doing this and even invite a conversation around this with your client is a whole other ball game. This is ethical, relational, private practice at its best!

Case Study: Nigel states in his contract that he is available daily between 9 am and 8 pm. He doesn't stipulate what type of contact he expects from clients but hopes that clients will just know to be "respectful". One night, at 9.15 pm, one of his clients Barbara, starts texting him. She feels anxious and wants to let him know and offload a little. Despite this being outside of his available hours, he answers her. He gives a few relatively short responses to a number of successive texts. The conversation ends, and Nigel thinks no more of it. He doesn't bring it up with her in the next session, nor in supervision. The week after, Barbara emails Nigel, stating that she wishes to discuss something in particular in the next session. This time the email is within his stated work hours, and Nigel responds thanking her for her email, and replying in a therapeutic manner. Again, he does not follow this up in the following session. Some weeks later, Barbara messages again – outside of his available hours, with similar content to the first exchange. When Nigel picks the message up, he immediately feels annoyed that Barbara is being disrespectful of his time. He picks up on his visceral sense of overwhelm and decides not to respond. When their next scheduled session arrives, Barbara is not there. He is left wondering what has happened, and although believes he was right to not respond based on how he felt, and it being outside of his stated working hours, he feels anxious that perhaps she has experienced it as hurtful.

Analysis: We might begin by asking what is Nigel's definition of respect, and what is Barbara's? His assumption that his understanding of this word fits with his clients, is misguided. It's up to us as therapists to be detailed and specific in practice boundaries so as not to cause confusion, as well as avoiding putting an unspoken expectation onto our clients, such as "don't disrespect me". Further, Nigel answered the first message outside of his own stated working hours, thereby breaking his own boundaries. Given he failed to follow up on this later with Barbara, it might not be unusual for Barbara to expect that she would receive a reply in their third exchange (in the same way she had for the first text). Finally, we are told that in the second exchange, Nigel has responded in a "therapeutic way", so has opened up the possibility of there being contact in this way. It appears he has progressed from short replies to her first text, to a full response in this second exchange. In short, there has been a lot of mixed messages from Nigel to Barbara about when (if), it is okay for her contact him; in what manner; and how often. Although we don't know why she hasn't turned up for the session, there is certainly the possibility that the confusion has caused hurt.

Case Study: Raefe, an integrative therapist, has it stated in his contract that he does not engage with clients in-between sessions. He has been working with Reuben for six weeks, when he receives an email from him, stating that he was "enjoying the work, but wondered why he had not been given any CBT techniques to use, and wondered if that could happen going forward". On this occasion, Raefe decides to bend his boundary and reply, thanking Reuben for his thoughts in empathic, relational way, and saying that he would look forward to talking about this in the next session.

Analysis: There's might be a few things that would need to be considered here, such as the need for an unbiased open curiosity from Raefe about the reasons why Reuben may have decided to email this question (as opposed to asking directly); how Reuben might be feeling about his therapy space; Raefe and Reuben's therapeutic and business relationship, especially with regards to expectations around the work (does Raefe even offer CBT therapy/have they discussed this previously?). Raefe has tried to act in a way that shows that he "sees" Reuben, by bending his boundary and replying in an empathic way, without opening the conversation up over email. In doing so, he manages to keep in place the frame of the therapeutic work, while not dismissing Reuben or being deflective, and protecting his own free time beyond this exchange.

This is an example of a non-punitive, and gentle way to address anything that pushes on stipulated boundaries. Remember, clients may not necessarily be pushing boundaries "on purpose"; there could be different therapeutic reasons why it is happening, or even simple practical explanations, such as the client just didn't remember what the contract said! Sometimes, a private practitioner can panic about why a client might be doing things outside of what the contract says, but it's important to find a grounded and relational position. We can continue to believe in, have confidence in, and enforce our practice boundaries while simultaneously relating to the client in an empathic way.

Practice boundaries – cancellation policy

Case study: Rita started her private practice three months ago. When she began to write her contract in preparation, she found setting the cancellation policy, the most challenging part. She was struggling to work out what was a "fair" policy. She discussed the issue with some of her contemporaries and posted the question in a large Facebook group, keen to find out what they had set as their own. In the end, she settled on a 48-hour cancellation policy, on the basis that others had suggested it. She has heard that it protects the therapist from losing too much money via last-minute cancellations, while also giving clients a reasonable amount of time to cancel if needed. This was written into her contract and communicated with all clients in the first session. At the six-session mark, one of her clients, Diane, cancelled on the day, telling Rita that she had a sinus infection. A few days go by, and Rita noticed that Diane has not paid for the missed session, despite it being under 48 hours (Rita asks her clients to pay on the day of their session). She feels very nervous about this, and wonders if she is being mean by expecting a client to pay for what she perceives as a nasty illness. When she next meets with Diane, neither party brings it up, and Diane does not pay. Rita decides to "write it off". Four weeks later, Diane cancels again on the day, this time advising her that she cannot come because she has a cold. A few days later, Rita is in supervision and mentions to her supervisor how cross she is, because Diane has again not mentioned anything about payment, and has not paid for the session. She doesn't see that a cold is worthy of non-payment of a session and says to her supervisor that as she feels her contract is clear to clients, she would like to proceed this time around, by pursuing the payment.

Exercise
What could be the ethical issue here? What are useful reflection points for Rita? What next steps would you take if you were her?

Practice boundaries – complaints

One part of your contract should include information about who you are registered with, and/or what ethical code you adhere to, as well as details about how a client can make a complaint about you. Complaints against a private practitioner need to be taken seriously. Sometimes, we may not realise the importance of a complaint, or not take it seriously until it gets to the level of "official" complain, that is, being lodged by the client, and carried forward with whatever body the practitioner belongs to. And that's not always due to flippancy, or not caring; often, it can be because complaints can feel very scary. And even more so to the private practitioner, who is working on their own. It can be tempting to hope that it will just go away. The best advice to private practitioners, though, is to take the complaint on headfirst and attempt to make amends and/or resolve (while working through your emotional process with your supervisor). Although the BACP framework does not mention private practice per se on this issue, there are up to three references, which indicate that we ought to be open to hearing feedback and discussing concerns with clients. They are as follows:

*BACP's Ethical Framework, Good Practice, point 15 (c) states:
"We will respect our clients as people by providing services that: c. Accept we are all vulnerable to prejudice and recognise the importance of self-inquiry, personal feedback and professional development" (BACP, 2018)

*BACP's Ethical Framework, Good Practice, point 49 states:
"We will encourage clients to raise any concerns about our work with them at the earliest possible opportunity, give any concerns careful consideration and, when appropriate, attempt to resolve them ...." (BACP, 2018)

*BACP's Ethical Frame work, Good Practice, 93 states:
"We will use supervision and any other available professional resources to support and challenge how we respond to such situations. We will give careful consideration to the best approaches to ethical problem-solving" (BACP, 2018).

In whatever way a client may experience us in the work, it is important to be open to that and hear them on it. As relational practitioners, this is part of respecting the client and taking seriously our commitment to any potential hurt that they have experienced. It means actively working as a therapist who is committed and dedicated to not increasing levels of distress, or minimising the impact of something that may have been inadvertent, or not done with intent. And it is crucial because carelessness in attending to initial complaints raised by clients can cause a secondary level of hurt, and is likely to be harmful. Notwithstanding serious breaches, and neglectful practice, the BACP is clear in their framework that professional/ethical issues, and problems and dilemmas are an unavoidable part of our practice. Perhaps as practitioners, we need to therefore be less fearful of this, and more open to our fallibleness as human beings, and the complexities of relational work. Except for the most extreme breaches, being aware that ethics often goes beyond purely what is a set list of "rights" and "wrongs" can help us when something goes wrong. It can remind us to be curious, to be humble, to be therapeutic, to be relational and to engage in a focussed process of ethical decision-making, as well as sensitive and caring in interactions with the said client. Often these interactions will happen within sessions, but if a client indicates they are not happy for whatever reason, and does not wish to continue with therapy, it would be prudent for the private practitioner to offer a free chat (with clear time boundaries laid out). Not charging for this conversation takes into consideration all the above, and also pays attention to issues around power and money. In other words, being mindful that charging a client to talk to you about harm they may feel they have experienced from you has the potential to make the client feel exploited. Sometimes, we might feel defensive, or reluctant to do this, especially if we think we haven't done anything wrong, or that a client's reaction to something we as the therapist have said or done was due to some kind of transference. However, we would want to be careful to not assume, and inadvertently move the responsibility onto the client. Petruska Clarkson's five relationship model talks about different levels that contribute to relational therapy, and so being mindful of things such as "the working alliance"; "the person to person relationship" and potentially "the reparative/developmentally needed relationship" can enable us to stay open-minded (Clarkson, 2003). Because we can never simply assume that we haven't made a mistake and it is "just transference". And even if it is transference, that still doesn't change how the client may have felt hurt, or any potential for our own countertransference, which might account for a mistake being made. Being open to all the possibilities when something goes wrong means acting with integrity as a practitioner. To offer up a short amount of free time is not incompatible with running a business either. On a practical level, it echoes many other businesses which would offer up such a space for someone who was not happy with something that they had received from a particular service.

TAKE-AWAY MESSAGES: A clear written contract, with well-thought-out practice boundaries, will fair you well. Take time to fully reflect of this crucial element of private practice.

References

BACP (2018). *Ethical framework for the counselling professions.* BACP. www.bacp.co.uk/media/3103/bacp-ethical-framework-for-the-counselling-professions-2018.pdf

Clarkson, P. (2003). *The therapeutic relationship* (2nd edn.). Whurr Publishers.

NCPS (2023). *Code of ethical practice.* NCPS. https://nationalcounsellingsociety.org/assets/uploads/docs/National-Counselling-Society-Code-of-Ethics.pdf

Travis, J. (Host), Binstead, C. (Guest), (2022). *How clear boundaries help you grow your practice, with Caz Binstead.* Grow Your Private Practice Show. www.janetra vis.co.uk/how-clear-boundaries-help-you-grow-your-private-practice-with-caz-binstead/

UKCP (2019). *UKCP code of ethics and professional practice.* UKCP. www.psycho therapy.org.uk/media/bkjdm33f/ukcp-code-of-ethics-and-professional-practice-2019.pdf

Williams, C. (2023). *Boundaries within the counselling profession.* BACP. www. bacp.co.uk/events-and-resources/ethics-and-standards/good-practice-in-action/publications/gpia110-boundaries-within-the-counselling-professions-fs/

Chapter 6

A brief overview of the different forms of online therapy and the respective ethical considerations

Nicholas Sarantakis and Caz Binstead

Online delivery of sessions has entered dynamically into the world of counselling and psychotherapy especially after the peak of the pandemic. A growing body of literature has been developing, which outlines the new opportunities and challenges that arise within this format of delivery. Nowadays, it is generally accepted that online delivery of therapy can be as effective as face-to-face therapy (e.g. Ierardi et al., 2022). Noteworthy research states that this is the case even when working with various forms of trauma, which is a sensitive area of work that needs to be contained very skilfully. For example, Turgoose et al. (2018) demonstrates in their systematic literature review that "tele-therapy" (including both video conference and audio-only sessions) can be equally effective even when working with ex-military veterans dealing with PTSD. Nonetheless, we should mention that the above body of research is based on long-established therapeutic approaches and not to newer models where the clinical and ethical implications of delivering them online are still largely unknown. Therefore, the private practitioner should be extremely reflective, and perhaps even cautious, when delivering interventions. Meanwhile, while arguably online delivery can be more inclusive to wider populations, we also need to be especially mindful of communicating effectively an anti-discriminatory stance to our clients (Sarantakis, 2017) in order to promote social justice, which may be more challenging online, given the absence of direct body language.

Even though online delivery has increased rapidly over the last years, the authors have observed that large numbers of clients are perhaps more inclined to prefer face-to-face sessions. This could be due to the extreme limitations of in-person contact that we all experienced during the height of the pandemic, but at the same time may also indicate that there are particular qualities relating to face-to-face sessions, which cannot be replaced with

DOI: 10.4324/9781003435624-6

online delivery. Therefore we believe that it is quite unlikely that the latter will totally override the traditional face-to-face sessions. There are several formats of online therapy today with the most common being the delivery of sessions via video conference. This format is the one that most resembles face-to-face sessions, as it entails a live face-to-face dialogue. Nonetheless, there are some obvious limitations, such as the fact that the body language of both the therapist and the client is not fully visible to one another. Despite such limitations, most authors writing on the subject nowadays do acknowledge that there are ways that these can be dealt with, and given the multiple other advantages of online therapy, they still generally endorse it and view it as an ethically appropriate format of delivery, albeit with specific recommendations. For example, Weinberg (2020) discusses such limitations for online therapeutic groups (where establishing cohesion and a working alliance can arguably be more challenging compared to face-to-face groups), and suggests that the therapist could be more active and use increased self-disclosure to compensate for the lack of physical presence.

Another form of online therapy is via online audio calls, which resemble phone counselling/emergency hotlines for mental health support which have of course been present for many years before the wide spread of the internet-based formats of delivery. The effectiveness of phone therapy has long been established through several studies over time, as the meta-analysis of Coughtrey and Pistrang (2018) demonstrates, and it is indeed very likely that this also applies to internet-based audio calls, which are practically very similar. There are, however, certain technical differences, which may have some ethical implications. For example, the cost of an online call is considerably lower, which is a clear advantage as it offers the opportunity to individuals around the world to reach a therapist of their choice for audio-based sessions in any different country, with a minimal cost. Furthermore, private practitioners have the advantage of being able to deliver any form of online therapy from their own home and through devices (such as smart phones and laptops) which arguably increases accessibility. Clinical experience of working with clients who feel especially vulnerable, or who are experiencing a current crisis, indeed indicate that they are more inclined to seek audio sessions as this provides them the distance they need, to speak to someone about their crisis without feeling the embarrassment that often accompanies face-to-face sessions for such clients. Despite these clear advantages, we should mention, though, that from a social justice and inclusivity perspective, it is still important to consider offering traditional phone sessions as an option, since – even today – some clients (especially of older generations) may not feel comfortable with online platforms, or, may not even have access to the internet.

It is paramount for the private practitioner offering online modalities to be very explicit – before committing to delivering therapy in such formats – about their boundaries, especially around their availability. And this is especially relevant to the next online format of delivery discussed here (therapy via texting), where some – especially younger clients – may misperceive it as being a form of befriending, as they are so used to texting actual friends (via social media), "virtual friends", and even people they barely know, at any time.

Sessions via texting is one of the most recent and controversial forms of delivery. It is often one of the options offered by online therapy platforms, and it is typically chosen by the younger population seeking to explore issues that they experience as embarrassing or shameful. Relevant research on this new mode is still scarce, not always of a high standard, and not free from bias or implicit commercial agendas, when promoted by online platforms offering such forms of therapy. However, it is worth mentioning that a systematic review of these few studies (Hoermann at al., 2017) shows generally positive outcomes for clients from synchronous text-based sessions, compared to individuals being on waiting lists, and also show equivalent (but not superior) outcomes compared to face-to-face or telephone therapy. While Dwyer et al. (2021) generally confirm the above findings and also stress that this format can be especially useful for individuals living in remote and rural areas and who are seeking an increased level of privacy and anonymity, they also highlight that often this is a way to identify individuals at risk, or in need of further, more targeted interventions. Such clients may instead need to be referred for face-to-face or video-based support. Therefore, while sessions via texting can definitely add social value to our profession, as it can offer access to people who would hesitate to seek therapy via other forms, we need to, again, be very mindful – especially as private practitioners – of being explicit about the professional boundaries and limitations, and will sometimes need to voice to certain clients that texting therapy may not be the most suitable option for them. Also, we must ensure that we use a safe and proper platform for therapy via texting, which is totally separate and unconnected to our personal and social media profiles, in order to avoid distracting or confusing our clients.

Therapy via texting can be synchronous or asynchronous. That means that it can either be a live texting conversation (synchronous), where the interaction is obviously much slower compared to all other formats, as both parties have to type their text to each other, without having any of the visual or audio cues, which would otherwise help establish psychological contact and provide better understanding of the context of each other's statements. Alternatively, asynchronous texting has the advantage that both parties can take their time to read and respond to each other, usually with longer texts, as, typically, the platforms that offer this format (or the private practitioner) set a certain frequency of text exchange (e.g. a client can "buy" a package of one text exchange with their therapist within 24 hours). This more resembles writing a letter to each other, rather than having a "live dialogue", as is the case with the most common forms of online therapy. Even though the authors acknowledge the potential value of this form of delivery, they would suggest that therapists engaging with asynchronous texting share more of their thinking process with the client, and remain tentative, instead of drawing quick conclusions or offering speedy interventions. This will hopefully help them to understand their clients better, and establish sufficient rapport with them. It may be a slower and more indirect process, which won't be suitable for all clients and all therapists, but at the same time, can become a very meaningful interaction for a client (which takes place on a regular basis).

The authors can generally see the potential value of this form of delivery, as certain clients would probably not seek therapy at all if this option was not available. Nonetheless, therapists need to be very mindful about the language they use in their texts so that it is not misperceived as insensitive or intrusive, given the lack of visual and audio contact. They would also need to be more cautious regarding any inferences, conclusions, or interventions that they may offer, as they can only rely on the written texts sent by the client. Thus, the inherent challenge is that despite the slow pace of interaction and the limited information to work with, we still need to establish rapport with the client and a sense of direction. Some clients may even expect quick and practical "tips" or techniques from the therapist, to help them with their issue, which the latter may have to resist offering, if they feel that they have not yet adequately understood their client's difficulty and life context. Indeed, this kind of "ethical awareness" is especially important in the "online texting therapy world", where the notion of instant gratification may be much more prominent.

Another interesting option (typically offered by online platforms and freelance practitioners who collaborate with them) are the "online drop-in" sessions. Practically, that means a therapist being available during a certain time window (usually for blocks of 30 minutes sessions of any online form), where any client may sign up to speak with them in-the-moment. This interaction might often be the first and last one between the specific client and therapist. Several private practitioners would object to this form of delivery, on the grounds that there would not be sufficient time to do anything meaningful with a "one-off client". However, there is also the argument that this is a more contemporary form of a mental health crisis hotline; the social value of which has been shown for decades now (the anonymous hotlines offered by the Samaritans in the UK is a good example of this, even if they do not provide a specialised psychological service as such).

In terms of the general advantages of the different forms of online therapy, probably the most obvious one is the easy access for clients (especially those who live in remote areas, or have a difficulty in commuting to meet their therapists) to a very broad range of practitioners that they would not be able to reach otherwise. And this can be really important for clients who seek highly specialised treatment, which may not be available in their geographical area (e.g. Stoll et al., 2020; Chakrabati, 2015). Furthermore, online therapy does not have the limitations of specific space and time availability, which means that the frequency, consistency and time of the sessions (or of texting, emails, etc.) can vary, and thus the therapist has the option to agree to meet the client's needs in a more flexible manner (Wodarski & Frimpong, 2013). This opportunity for increased flexibility is actually not just a practical manner, but it could challenge the traditional notion of boundaries (e.g. sessions have to be weekly, for 50 minutes each, and at the same time via an in- person verbal interaction). Therefore, although boundaries are of course essential for both clinical and ethical reasons, the therapist may agree with their online clients, a different framework of boundaries, for good reasons. For example, several clients sometimes feel that the time of a specific session is not enough, while in other sessions, they may barely have anything to talk about. In such cases, the online delivery makes other alternatives (e.g. ad hoc sessions, which may vary in terms of duration as well) much easier and this could also serve both the client and the therapist better. The increased access which online therapy provides, can also be beneficial in terms of potentially avoiding possibly awkward situations in small towns or villages, where it is quite likely that clients will come across their therapists by coincidence (for example at the local supermarket or pub), or in other social events (e.g. in the local Church, or in the local sports club). Although normally private practitioners, especially in small communities, will have discussed very explicitly with their clients in advance what should happen if they meet each other by coincidence outside of the therapy room (e.g. do they want to be acknowledged or not, especially in the presence of other people as well), this does not mean that such instances cannot still be awkward for both the client and therapist. Although, it's worth noting, that this doesn't completely solve the 'problem', as we need to still be mindful that clients and practitioners alike are increasingly participating in several online communities, social media and discussion fora, the content of which cannot always be kept private. Regarding such spaces, it probably good ethical practice for us as private practitioners to avoid 'checking' the online presence of their clients, as such information (and possibly any conscious, or unconscious bias that we may develop about them based on this information) may influence the therapeutic work that we do with them. However, it would be unreasonable to ask our clients 'not to check us online', as we do have a major influence in their lives and they may have the natural curiosity to know more about us. By the same token, we may want as practitioners to exercise our freedom to participate in a public online discussion about mental health, or any other topic. While therapists who work for organisations do have to consider carefully, the possible impact of their online presence for their organisations, private practitioners arguably have more autonomy, freedom and responsibility when making such decisions. It makes it even more important therefore, to be ever mindful of the possible impact of our online presence to those clients who come across it (see Chapter 11 for more reflections around social media).

The convenience of online video conferences, means that some practitioners might offer a free, short trial to clients to help them and the client decide whether they want to commit to regular sessions. Given the sometimes, impersonal nature of professional websites and email correspondence, this could indeed be good ethical practice, and offers the opportunity to therapists as well, to form an opinion on whether they feel comfortable working with a particular prospective client, and/or, if the piece of work is within their area of expertise, or level of competence. That said, it's worth remembering of course, that in general, there are arguments for and against offering free initial sessions, and it's important for private practitioners to consider all the options, and decide what works best for them (as discussed in Chapter 5).

Probably the most important disadvantage of online therapy is the limited control that the therapist can exercise over important elements of ethical practice. For example, they cannot have total control over the security and privacy of the online communication tools they use, they cannot know how private the space is where the client is located during the online session, or they may not know adequately the identity, age, legal, ethical and cultural context of a client, especially when the latter is located in a different country. Many private practitioners nowadays choose to collaborate with various organisations and platforms, which may take care to different degrees of such ethical and technical matters on their behalf. However, the therapists who work completely independently (and thus hold full clinical and professional responsibility) will need to obtain as much relevant information as possible about a prospective online client, before deciding to work (or not) with them. This discussion links with the question of whether formal training is necessary for delivering online therapy. While as private practitioners, we can certainly benefit from such trainings, and from liaising with more experienced online practitioners, we should also be mindful that not all trainings offered commercially, can add something substantial to what we can learn from colleagues, or on our own, with supervisory support.

Overall, even though the online delivery of therapy is now undeniably a big part of the landscape of our profession, deciding what form of delivery feels right for us and under what circumstances, always remains a personal choice for both therapists and clients.

TAKE-AWAY MESSAGES: Remember to consider the overall advantages and disadvantages around online therapy, and its various formats (video conference, audio sessions, synchronous and asynchronous texting, and online drop-in sessions). This will help you to reflect on the different ethical considerations involved.

References

Chakrabarti S. (2015). Usefulness of telepsychiatry: A critical evaluation of videoconferencing-based approaches. *World Journal of Psychiatry*, 5(3), 286–304. doi: 10.5498/wjp.v5.i3.286

Coughtrey, A. E., Pistrang, N. (2018). The effectiveness of telephone-delivered psychological therapies for depression and anxiety: A systematic review. *Journal of Telemedicine and Telecare*, 24(2), 65–74. doi: 10.1177/1357633X16686547

Dwyer, A., De Almeida Neto, A., Estival, D., Li, W., Lam-Cassettari, C., Antoniou, M. (2021). Suitability of text-based communications for the delivery of psychological therapeutic services to rural and remote communities: Scoping review. *Journal of Medical Internet Research*, 8(2), e19478. doi: 10.2196/19478

Hoermann, S., McCabe, K. L., Milne, D. N., Calvo, R. A. (2017). Application of synchronous text-based dialogue systems in mental health interventions: Systematic review. *Journal of Medical Internet Research*, 19(8), e267. doi: 10.2196/jmir.7023

Ierardi, E., Bottini, M., Riva Crugnola, C. (2022). Effectiveness of an online versus face-to-face psychodynamic counselling intervention for university students before and during the COVID-19 period. *BMC Psychology*, 10, 35. https://doi.org/10.1186/s40359-022-00742-7

Sarantakis, N. P. (2017). Reflections on an anti-discriminatory practice in current psychotherapy. *Journal of Contemporary Psychotherapy*, 47(2), 135–140. doi: 10.1007/s10879-016-9353-4

Stoll, J., Muller, J. A., Trachsel, M. (2020). Ethical issues in online psychotherapy: A narrative review. *Frontiers in Psychiatry*, 10, 993. https://doi.org/10.3389/fpsyt.2019.00993

Turgoose, D., Ashwick, R., Murphy D. (2018). Systematic review of lessons learned from delivering tele-therapy to veterans with post-traumatic stress disorder. *Journal of Telemedicine and Telecare*, 24(9), 575–585. doi: 10.1177/1357633X17730443

Weinberg, H. (2020). Online group psychotherapy: Challenges and possibilities during COVID-19—A practice review. *Group Dynamics: Theory, Research, and Practice*, 24(3), 201–211. doi: 10.1037/gdn0000140

Wodarski, J., Frimpong, J. (2013). Application of e-therapy programs to the social work practice. *Journal of Human Behavior in the Social Environment*, 23(1), 29–36. doi: 10.1080/10911359.2013.737290

Chapter 7

Ethics in couple's, family, and group therapy in private practice

Nicholas Sarantakis and Caz Binstead

Why is the three-dimensional model important in these modalities?

In this book we have introduced the "three-dimensional model", which we believe can be useful in terms of analysing and understanding the ethical dilemmas and challenges that may arise in private therapy practice. We believe that this model is particularly useful when used in couple's, family, and group therapy, as there are more parties involved within these therapeutic modalities (and thus the relational dynamics are more complex), and also because the formal ethical codes do not actually provide sufficient guidelines or insights about how to manage ethical challenges and dilemmas within this context (Shaw, 2015). Furthermore, research shows that, generally, practitioners tend to seek support for their work mostly from supervisors or senior colleagues (Doyle & Miller, 2009), rather than relying primarily on formal ethical codes (Congress & McAuliffe, 2006). Even in more recent years, a systematic review which explored how clinical psychologists (and mental health practitioners more generally) make ethical decisions, indicates that there is a clear gap in the literature on this area, with them suggesting that future research should consider not only the formal ethical codes, but also the therapist's personal factors (such as personal beliefs, and the therapist's perception of their clients), as things which influence their ethical decision-making-process (Grace et al., 2020). All the above support one of the fundamental premises of this book, which is that while ethical codes are generally quite generic, which of course comes with various advantages, we also need to acknowledge the inevitable role of the therapist's personal factors, as well as the context of the therapeutic work, and apply a reflective and interpersonal stance, when faced with ethical dilemmas.

DOI: 10.4324/9781003435624-7

When more than one client is involved within the same therapeutic process, and especially when these clients are related to each other, as partners or as a family, the therapist will often have to consider very carefully how they make decisions that balance – in the best possible manner – the values, aims, and interests of each of these clients involved in therapy. They will need to consider carefully what could possibly be best for them as a unit (e.g. family or couple); the therapist's own aims and therapeutic philosophy as practitioners, along with other wider considerations (e.g. other members in the family who do not partake in therapy, formal ethics codes, insurance companies, and the broader social and cultural considerations). As we have discussed in the introduction, and seen throughout this book in practice, the main hypothesis of the three-dimensional model we have proposed, is that ethical dilemmas and challenges typically arise as a conflict or tension between the different values and subjective aims of three different parties involved in therapy, namely the client, the therapist and the wider context and society. When we consider subjectivity in this setting though, we have to be aware of some potential challenges that could lead to obvious ethical issues, and keep in mind that the overarching, universal ethical values of counselling and psychotherapy (and of society more generally) should be prioritised above and beyond individual subjective aims of the therapist or the individual clients. For example, if the therapist is having a "secret" one-to-one therapeutic relationship with one family member, without the knowledge of the other family members, who are involved in family therapy, this could clearly damage the trust of the family, with each other and in relation to the therapeutic process. Alternatively, if a family member is being physically or psychologically violent towards other members of the family, this is obviously not acceptable and has to be recognised in the therapeutic space, regardless of what the aggressive person believes, or where the other partner, or the family unit, may implicitly regard such behaviours as "normal". Thus, such examples, can be considered as clear ethical problems, and require even more careful and balanced thinking when applying the three-dimensional model. Indeed, private practitioners, as well as practitioners who work for organisations, base their work on certain universal values, such as the promotion of healthy relationships in couples and families and, of course, the overall psychological wellbeing of all parties. Thus, when there is a clear risk of these values being compromised, this risk cannot be overshadowed by the possible disparity of individual views, or the individual aims of each party. Having said that, it is also true that there is a vast "grey area" in ethical decision-making, where the subjective aims and values of each party in therapy may be different or even incompatible, but at the same time, they can all be seen as legitimate and important, if we view them through the lenses of each individual. It is in such cases, where we need to equally acknowledge and value all these different perspectives, that our "three-dimensional model" is particularly useful and applicable. As mentioned above, this model recognises three different parties involved in therapy, namely the client, the therapist, and the wider context/ society, but within the context of couple and family therapy, the party of the "client" would most often entail further possible division of aims and values, that the therapist will have to consider carefully in their ethical decision-making. We shall now look more closely at these three dimensions, and how the dynamic between them may unfold in couple and family therapy.

The first dimension: the client(s)

We will start by exploring the ethics in couple's therapy, where, from the perspective of this framework, there are actually two dimensions within the party of "the client". It may be the case that the couple who comes to therapy have agreed in advance what they are seeking to achieve. However, in reality, they will most likely have different understandings of their goals, and what achieving them would look like. There are often implicit and disparate agendas between the two individuals in the relationship that are rarely expressed openly, at least during the initial sessions, or the parties may not even be fully aware of them. Most couple's therapists would agree that unravelling such "implicit agendas" would be a critical, if not essential, underlying component of the therapeutic process. In any case, each of the individuals involved in couples therapy will probably have a broad idea of what they want to achieve through their sessions (their subjective aims), and even when they are not so clear about that, they will know when they feel satisfied with their therapy. They may sometimes not have a very particular preconception about what exact "methods" they would expect their therapist to "apply" when working with them, but they will somehow know when their therapy meets their expectations and also – at a more implicit level – when their therapy is aligned with their values about how they want to work with their therapist and what they evaluate as "positive change" in their psychological wellbeing. The partners (clients) may agree on their therapeutic goals and with the therapist's methods for achieving them. However, they may also have minor or major disagreements between them in their individual aims, so it would be useful for the therapist to provide some structure to the process, giving them both the opportunity to be heard and not "feel lost" (as it may happen when they are conversing without the presence of the therapist).

The second dimension: the therapist

In fact, the therapist will also have their own subjective aims and values, which means a "belief system" about what constitutes positive change and what are the most "vital ingredients" in their work. For example, a common axis upon which therapists position themselves is the extent to which they prioritise the "right therapeutic relationship" vs. the "right therapeutic tools". Arguably there has now been a large body of research on common factors in therapy which has consistently shown that the therapeutic relationship is a more critical factor than the choice of a particular therapeutic model or tools (as the classical "Lamber Pie", Asay and Lambert, 1999, has shown us). Even though this is an ongoing academic and professional discussion and debate (e.g. Cuijpers et al., 2019), it is evidently an area where the philosophy of practitioners can vary substantially and thus, they will bring this factor into the therapy room with their clients. Meanwhile, it would probably be unfair to label any stance within this spectrum of therapeutic philosophy as more ethical than any other one. However, it would probably be good ethical practice to be aware of where we stand as therapists in this spectrum of "relationship vs. evidence-based techniques" and how the stance we hold is inevitably always at play in our work with clients. Thus, from this perspective, practising ethically could mean that we are transparent and open both with ourselves and clients regarding our therapeutic philosophy. Even if the couple or family has a different view about what they feel they need, the therapist's explanation of their therapeutic philosophy could potentially help them view things from a new, more helpful perspective. However, private practitioners should also reflect on whether their own – legitimate – confidence in their approach may override unduly the expressed needs and agenda of their clients.

Meanwhile, conflict of aims or values may also arise within the therapists themselves, and making the best possible decision, given the limited information we have at each moment, could be a challenge, especially when these contrasting aims and values can be seen as equally significant. For example, in family therapy, a therapist could be faced with a situation where one family member discloses a secret to them, and the therapist finds themselves faced with the ethical challenge of trying to wisely balance the value of confidentiality with potentially other factors (depending on the situation, and/or family member involved), such as duty of care. Moreover, regarding the therapist's own aims and values, these can also be distinguished in two different main categories. The first one concerns the therapist's own predisposition about personal relationships, which would inevitably be at play in their work with couples. This essentially has to do with whether a practitioner is most inclined to promote reconciliation within the couple (and thus towards finding "solutions" that could be implemented in their daily lives to help them avoid unnecessary conflict), or whether they think that conflicts within the couple should be uncovered and explored in depth, believing that if the eventual outcome for the couple is separation, probably this would be unavoidable anyway in the long-term. In such cases, the most ethical stance for the therapist would probably be to listen very carefully to what the couple (and the individuals involved) want to gain from therapy and try to agree with both of them on a minimum ground of therapeutic goals (e.g. do they both agree they want to try to "save" the relationship?), and then consider carefully what approach would be best for them, while bracketing – as much as possible – their personal beliefs and predispositions about relationships. In any case, the practitioner will most likely find themselves in delicate situations where they will need to consider very carefully if they should voice any (tentative) hypotheses they may have formed about the implicit agenda of each of the partners in the couple, how to communicate such hypotheses and what would be the impact of sharing them in the "micro-system" of the couple. Moreover, should they decide to share their hypotheses, they would also have to consider what would be the optimal verbal and non-verbal language they use, so that they most likely provoke constructive rather than negative reactions to the couple. And this language of course would also have to be congruent with the therapist's own values and therapeutic style, while being respectful to the prevailing cultural norms.

The third dimension: the wider context

By the term wider context, particularly in couple and family therapy, we mean other factors, such as:

• The other members of the family that may not partake in therapy, but are nevertheless affected indirectly by it.

- The ethos and culture of the professional group that each practitioner belongs to (i.e. the modality they practice and whether they are counsellors, psychotherapists, counselling or clinical psychologists, even though in reality there is extensive overlap).
- The formal ethical codes that the practitioner may adhere to.
- The practitioner's supervisor (or/and, in certain occasions, their peer-led supervision group).
- Other parties, such as insurance companies, agencies, clinics, or platforms that may mediate between the therapist and their clients and so on.
- Society as a whole, which includes wider social norms, and, social issues. Consideration of how this affects, or inter-relates with the other dimensions, i.e., the circumstances, or cultural identities, of the therapist, or clients (family, couple, or individual member of either).

Even though the impact of this third dimension is normally indirect and sometimes not so obvious, we argue that it is important to consider, as we need to honour the expectations of such third parties and sometimes these can be in contrast with the other two dimensions mentioned above (the client and the therapist). For example, an individual client may have been referred to a private practitioner by their insurance company, but after some one-to-one sessions, the direction of therapy could make the therapist feel that it would be beneficial to invite another member of the family for a number of sessions, in order to explore certain vital family dynamics. However, insurance companies generally authorise one-to-one sessions for the individual and not couple or family sessions (especially those ones who operate on the basis of diagnostic categories and the corresponding "treatment" for them). Thus, even though the therapist may see the benefit of integrating a few family or couple sessions within the work with their individual client, and the latter may suggest to the therapist to proceed with this approach informally without the insurance company, this could indeed be an ethical issue, as it would violate the agreed contract with the insurance company. Another example would be when two spouses decide to keep living together, but only as co-parents (while they agree to feel free to date other people, since they regard that they cannot rectify their romantic relationship), and they believe that this would be in the best interest of their children. The therapist, after having a few sessions of couple's therapy with the parents, may form the professional opinion that the psychological cost of such an arrangement for their children would be greater than any possible benefit of their parents staying (just as co-parents) together. However, although we as practitioners understandably form such personal and professional opinions constantly, it would be best ethical practice to be mindful of the impact of what we communicate to our clients and in what way. In this example, the practitioner may form an opinion about the impact of such an arrangement to the children of the couple, but they would also need to respect the parents' autonomy, while inviting them to explore together openly and without prejudice the implications of differing possible arrangements on their children.

Structuring the process in an ethically-balanced manner

One of the authors, Nicholas, who is working regularly with couples and families, would suggest planning the following stages (steps), as a way of providing some structure to the couple, but also as a way of ensuring – as much as possible – that the private practitioner manages the process in the most ethical manner possible. These steps would entail:

i)   Exploring initially through one-to-one single sessions with each partner their individual subjective narrative and aims.
ii) Identifying during the first joint session any common themes that they both agree to work on (even if they have different perspectives about why the problems occurred, or what is the way forward).
iii) Working on the most immediate or relatively simple problem.
iv) Working through issues that are particularly important for one of them, once some trust has been built for the process and they are both more willing to listen to each other and acknowledge their individual needs.
v)   And, possibly supporting each other in processing their individual unresolved "historical emotional baggage" with the sensitive guidance of the therapist. This would need an enhanced level of mutual empathy and understanding that often partners do and say things to each other that can be hurtful – not necessarily because they intend to hurt their feelings, but because of their own inner conflicts and sensitivities (which are also triggered by "something" that their partner does). The reality is of course that many couples (or families) may never be ready to reach this stage, as when they come for therapy, they often have a history of events in their relationship, which can be very difficult to "forgive". It has to be acknowledged that is it often quite challenging (but not impossible!) for

couples to develop this enhanced level of empathy for each other. Thus, the therapist has to be receptive and sensitive in their understanding of where the couple (or family unit) stands at each moment. Insisting on such an agenda can leave one (or sometimes both) of the parties feeling that the therapist implies that they should "forgive" or accept in some way certain behaviours from their partner, which have been deeply hurtful and/or in sharp contrast with their own values and beliefs about what a romantic relationship, marriage, or family life should be like. Given these limitations, such in-depth therapeutic work can nevertheless be valuable, as seminal and more recent research has shown that positive romantic relationships have the potential – over time – to help with changing avoidant or insecure attachment styles usually deriving from childhood (e.g. Bayraktaroglu, 2023; Arriana et al., 2018).

The above described process means that as therapists we validate the aims and agenda of both parties in the couple (while remaining neutral, as much as possible, about "what is really the problem here"); we facilitate the couple or family to find the very minimum of common ground between themselves, and help them to develop a step-by-step deepening of a mutual understanding and mutually agreed ways forward. Simultaneously, this could also be a way for balancing the power between the therapist and the clients and between the clients themselves, and this can indeed be empowering for them. It is also ethical practice in the sense that it mitigates against the risk of the therapy being experienced by any parties as not impartial, due to the management of the process, or due to the therapist's own preconceptions, values, or personal experiences.

The factor of power in couple and family therapy

Who holds most of the power in couple/family therapy and how can we manage this dimension in an ethical manner? Below are some considerations around this:

- Sometimes the person in the couple or family who wants to maintain the unit the most and at all costs would hold less power, as they would be more willing to accept the other person's agenda in therapy, in order to save the relationship. In such cases, while of course we would want to honour the subjective aims of each party and how they each wish to approach the sessions, it could often be useful to offer the opportunity to this person who is willing to compromise too much (in order to save the relationship) to voice their needs as well, in a way that feels constructive, and at a time that they are ready to do so.

• The partner with "more power" at home often has more power in the couple's sessions as well and probably a stronger say on whether they should continue therapy or not, and they probably also aim to maintain this power within therapy and attempt to impose their own agenda (typically arguing that their partner needs to change their behaviour). Furthermore, their partner may sometimes collude with them, as they have already accepted their power at home, and maybe they have also accepted that they are indeed the "problem" in the relationship and the reason they need therapy. Meanwhile, power dynamics from the couple's social, psychological, and financial relationship may be brought into therapy as well. We should not assume that the individual who instigates therapy necessarily holds more power "at home". For example, it could be the case that one of the partners instigates therapy because their partner is considering leaving the relationship and they do not want to do so themselves, so in this case the former would have less power. It may be one of the partners convincing the other that therapy could help them, but the other partner may hold more power at home, in terms of their financial contribution to the family, their professional status, in terms of their age difference, or the implicit comparison of their "perceived attractiveness", all of which are very delicate matters of power that the therapist may observe discretely, but may not mention, until the couple brings them up themselves, directly or indirectly.

• The therapist may find themselves in a conflicted position in terms of their own power and also in terms of managing the power dynamics within this complex system. They may wish to keep the couple in therapy with the best of intentions, as they believe that therapy will help them, and they have confidence in their own ability as professionals. In fact, they may do this unconsciously to some extent and they may use their power and authority to keep the couple or family in therapy for some time, without necessarily producing any real therapeutic benefit. Thus, especially in private practice, where clients pay privately and have more flexibility to return to therapy whenever they wish, it would be important to review periodically with our clients where they stand at each time and encourage them to take ownership of the direction and length of their sessions, while also providing them with honest feedback, when we are asked to do so.

Overall, it is generally accepted that ethical practice means honouring the autonomy and agency of clients and this would of course apply to both parties in the couple or all members of the family.

- Sometimes the therapist may intentionally, but gently, try to shift the power within this system in order to give the opportunity to the "Identified Patient", i.e. the scapegoat (as they are seen by the others in the system), to voice their own needs and eventually try to restore the power imbalance. Power imbalance (in this case between the members of the couple or family) can often cause ethical issues and thus it is reasonable to assume that promoting a balance of power during the sessions will most likely also help our clients to have healthier and more satisfying relationships at home. However, we need to be very careful with this area of work, as trying to shift the balance of power in the couple or family system could be perceived as a threat to their "system", if not done in a sensitive manner for all, and at the right timing (and this right timing may actually never arrive for certain clients). The individuals with more power in their system (couple or family) may become very resistant to such a change and they may convince their partner or family to end therapy prematurely, before any meaningful therapeutic gain has been achieved.

Some ethical considerations in group therapy

While group therapy can offer different, more relational benefits to clients, compared with individual therapy which seems to promote better emotional awareness, insights, and individual problem-solving (Holmes & Kivlighan, 2000), both modalities produce comparable therapeutic outcomes (e.g. Bastien, 2004). Group therapy is a more cost-effective modality, but it is also a way to fight loneliness and isolation. Phenomena that are becoming more frequent in Western societies, and are also correlated with several other health risk factors for older and middle-aged adults (e.g. National Academies of Sciences, Engineering and Medicine, 2020). Therefore, group therapy may become more common in the future, depending on its compatibility with the local culture and community life, and it is more likely that private practitioners will be offering this modality more in the future, and thus will have to deal with the relevant complex ethical dilemmas. One such important decision therapists need to make is an informed opinion about whether individual, family, or group therapy would most likely be the best option for each client(s) and their presenting issues (see a relevant discussion in Sarantakis, 2016).

Similarly with couple and family therapy, the therapist has to be conscious and consider the subjective aims and values of more than one client, but of course in group therapy, it's slightly different in that the clients are not related to each other in any personal way. There are occasions in community or inpatient settings where the clients will know each other and they may also share several other activities, however in private practice group therapy, it is most likely that the members of the group will meet each other for the first time during the first group session. Normally the rules and principles which will govern the group sessions will have to be discussed and agreed in advance with each individual member, however each of them will still bring their own personal meaning of the group process and their own agenda. Thus, even though the therapist would normally show equal interest and encourage all members to use the space, the members will inevitably have different personalities and thus some will be more dominant, while others will be more agreeable or more silent, and so on. Therefore, finding a way to balance such complex dynamics is not only a matter of technique, but also an ethical matter with broader implications: is it better for the therapist to stay more distant and neutral and allow the interpersonal dynamics to unfold within the group space as they would develop naturally in real social settings? Or would it be better if they take a more proactive role and intervene to balance the power in the group, give voice to the more silent members, and protect the more vulnerable and less confident in the group? How much competition or conflict should they allow in the group (so as to build resilience for the "real world") vs. intentionally fostering cohesion, solidarity, and care? It may be possible for a talented and experienced therapist to do both, however it would be important, as good ethical practice, for the therapist to be self-aware about their own core beliefs about whether growth happens more through developing resilience for dealing with difficulties and conflict, or more, through cultivating supportive relationships and avoiding tensions. This aspect concerns how the therapist facilitates a "process group", but inevitably such interpersonal dynamics will be present in some form in most groups, either explicitly or implicitly, as the members will bring different personalities and needs.

Other important ethical issues in group therapy concern confidentiality and relationships between group members that may develop as they get to know each other better through the group process. Regarding confidentiality, within the group context, the reality is that confidentiality and out-of-group contact cannot be guaranteed, even if the therapist sets such rules from the beginning. This is a limitation that is different compared to individual therapy, where keeping confidentiality (with the given limitations) depends solely on the therapist, who has an ethical duty to do so, as well as keeping professional boundaries regarding social contact with their clients. On the contrary, within a group context, both the therapist and the whole group will have to accept that the confidentiality of any sensitive disclosures relies not only on the therapist, but also on the mutual trust and adherence of all members to the "ground rules" and this should be clearly communicated (probably in writing) to everyone before their engagement with group sessions. Regarding out-of-group contact, traditionally (especially in group analysis and process groups) this would be prohibited, or at least strongly discouraged. However, some authors and clinicians suggest that if and when it happens, it should be openly shared with the whole group during the sessions (e.g. Flapan & Fenchel, 1983). In fact, it could be said that out-of-group contact can be a way for members to extend the solidarity expressed to each other during the sessions (even though some members make out-of-group contact for other reasons), and thus the therapist should not discourage it. This issue is just one of several examples, where the clinical research and ethics literature is still contentious, and it cannot provide definite answers. Therefore, in such dilemmas, the private practitioner may consider them on an ad hoc basis using the three-dimensional model as a framework to reach an optimal decision for all parties concerned.

Couple's therapy example

Case study: A couple comes to therapy because the husband has had an affair, and his wife found out. She wants to understand why he did it and how they can move on. After an intense session where the couple argue over this, the man emails the therapist, blaming him and stating that he took the side of his wife. He says that if that continues, he will stop paying for the sessions, meaning they will have to stop (the implication being that they can afford therapy, only because he is paying). The therapist is wondering whether they should continue with the sessions, and whether he should bring anything up during the joint sessions.

Analysis: While the wife's aim and hope seems to be to find a way to restore the trust in her husband and save their marriage, her husband seems to feel threatened by the possibility of losing his power over his wife and over therapy as well. Especially, since the therapist invited him not to be afraid to visit his own emotional vulnerability (dimension of clients). Meanwhile, the therapist felt unsafe by his behaviour, and at a personal level would want to discontinue therapy (dimension of therapist). Concurrently, he feels a duty of care towards the couple and does not want to abandon the work. He also wonders (based on this aggressive interaction) if there is a possibility that the husband may be emotionally abusive towards his wife (wider context dimension). Which of these conflicting aims is more important? The therapist could decide that, overall, the scope of the broader benefit (third dimension) is more important, and thus continue working with them, even though he feels uncomfortable. One final consideration is if he needs to share the husband's email in the next session (when both parties are present) and point out that it made him feel uncomfortable. Although, to do so would possibly damage the couple's relationship, and the prospects of couple's therapy as well.

Action: The therapist eventually decides to respond politely to the husband, stating they are sorry that the latter feels this way, that they never had any intention to take any sides, and encourage him to bring his concerns into the joint sessions himself. Should the husband refuse to do so, the therapist could wait to see what will happen in the next session, and see if he can help the husband build trust and openness in the therapeutic process. When considering power dynamics, it feels important that the wife is not "forgotten", and the therapist remains equally invested in her, and mindful of her own wellbeing.

TAKE-AWAY MESSAGES: In this chapter, we briefly explored how the three-dimensional model could be applied flexibly in couple's, family, and group therapy, while considering the specificities of these modalities, in addition to issues around power. We hope this stimulates you, the private practitioner, to reflect creatively on such issues.

References

Arriaga, X. B., Kumashiro, M., Simpson, J. A., Overall, N. C. (2018). Revising working models across time: Relationship situations that enhance attachment security. *Personality and Social Psychology Review*, 22(1), 71–96.

Asay, T. P., Lambert, M. J. (1999). The empirical case for the common factors in therapy: Quantitative findings. In Hubble, M. A., Duncan, B. L., Miller, S. D.

(Eds.), *The heart and soul of change: What works in therapy* (pp. 23–55). American Psychological Association. https://psycnet.apa.org/record/1999-02137-001

Bastien, C. H., Morin, C. M., Ouellet, M.-C., Blais, F. C., Bouchard, S. (2004). Cognitive-behavioral therapy for insomnia: Comparison of individual therapy, group therapy, and telephone consultations. *Journal of Consulting and Clinical Psychology*, 72(4), 653–659. https://doi.org/10.1037/0022-006X.72.4.653

Bayraktaroglu, D., Gunaydin, G., Selcuk, E., Besken, M., Karakitapoglu-Aygun, Z. (2023). The role of positive relationship events in romantic attachment avoidance. *Journal of Personality and Social Psychology*, 124(5), 958–970. https://doi.org/10.1037/pspi0000406

Congress, E., McAuliffe, D. (2006) Social work ethics: Professional codes in Australia and the United States. *International Social Work*, 49, 151. doi: 10.1177/0020872806061211

Cuijpers, P., Reijnders, M., Huibers, M. J. H. (2019). The role of common factors in psychotherapy outcomes. *Annual Review of Clinical Psychology*, 15, 207–231. doi: 10.1146/annurev-clinpsy-050718-095424

Doyle, O. Z., Miller, S. E. (2009). Ethical decision making in social work: Exploring personal and professional values. *Journal of Social Work Values and Ethics*, 6(1), 4–36.

Flapan, D., Fenchel, G. H. (1983). Group member contacts without the group therapist. Group 7, 3–16. https://doi.org/10.1007/BF01456439

Grace, B., Wainwright, T., Solomons, W., Camden, J., Ellis-Caird, H. (2020). How do clinical psychologists make ethical decisions? A systematic review of empirical research. *Clinical Ethics*, 15(4), 213–224. doi:10.1177/1477750920927165

Holmes, S. E., Kivlighan, D. M., Jr. (2000). Comparison of therapeutic factors in group and individual treatment processes. *Journal of Counseling Psychology*, 47(4), 478–484. https://psycnet.apa.org/doiLanding?doi=10.1037%2F0022-0167.47.4.478

National Academies of Sciences, Engineering and Medicine (2020). *Social isolation and loneliness in older adults: Opportunities for the Health Care System*. National Academies Press. https://doi.org/10.17226/25663

Sarantakis, N. P. (2016). Family or group therapy for cancer patients? An exploration of different ways of working and the inherent challenges therein. *Contemporary Psychotherapy*, 8(1). www.researchgate.net/publication/305114501_Understanding_Families_and_Groups_as_Systems_Family_or_group_therapy_for_cancer_patients_An_exploration_of_different_ways_of_working_and_the_inherent_challenges_therein_Nicholas_P_Sarantakis

Shaw, E. (2015). Ethical practice in couple and family therapy: Negotiating rocky terrain. *Australian and New Zealand Journal of Family Therapy*, 36(45), 504–517. doi: 10.1002/anzf.1129

Chapter 8

Social awareness in contemporary practice

Caz Binstead and Nicholas Sarantakis

We have spoken a lot in this book about how we are all unique individuals within our roles as private practitioners, and it is this very concept that makes this chapter so imperative and meaningful. People are all different. Read that again – PEOPLE ARE ALL DIFFERENT! This is a fact that we cannot get away from, and working with this is an intrinsic part of our work as therapists. Social awareness in contemporary practice refers to an ability to empathise with the needs of others, and to seek to hear and understand the diverse range of individuals' lived experiences, as members of society – even if they are very different to our own. Furthermore, it is an acknowledgement that our clients can, and will be, impacted by social factors that play out in wider society.

In humility, we would like to acknowledge that we do not have the space to cover every element of this crucial topic that needs discussing. But not including it was not an option. Seeing clients in who they are, and giving everyone that we work with dignity by acknowledging through our actions their right to "be" is in line with basic human rights. In the context of private practice, we need to ensure, therefore, that we are delivering equitable services to our clients, which honours anti-discriminatory practice; pays attention to our own assumptions and prejudices; and considers, carefully and thoughtfully, the ethics around creating culturally sensitive practices.

In line with our three-dimensional model, we will also be interested in the cultural diversity of private practitioners themselves. Part of this (amongst other considerations) will include a very relevant social issue when it comes to private practice – the role of money.

A changing field

The idea that counselling and psychotherapy should be apolitical has existed in the field for decades. Sadly, what this perspective fails to

DOI: 10.4324/9781003435624-8

recognise is that many of the structures of oppression which our clients may present with in the counselling and psychotherapy room have often been not just defined but reinforced by the political structures of the day.

(Turner, 2023, p. 32)

Although arguments calling for greater acknowledgement of the relevance of the social and political in the therapy room have slowly been becoming more mainstream over the years, certain incidences over the last few years have begun to seriously challenge previous assumptions. Factors such as the Covid-19 pandemic, the Black Lives Matter movement, the subject of climate change, and so on, have organically changed the way we interact with clients around "big" subjects that affect us all. We have been through an extraordinary process, where we really have all been in together, bringing to the surface in an overt way that therapists live in the very self-same world as clients. From a relational standpoint, it means we cannot be ignorant or remain entirely neutral to injustices and dangers that we all face as fellow human beings in a global world. The authors observed that when Covid-19 hit, it produced an intense, yet more truthful process in the therapy space. It was a unique time when both therapist and client sat facing each other in full knowledge that *both* parties were experiencing something life-changing and scary. This is, of course, a more known phenomenon in therapy, where familiar experiences between the therapist and client might be noted by the former, with the crucial difference being, *that the client doesn't know.*

Building a permissive space

As practitioners engaging with relational ethics, we have no choice but to consider how we adapt to these evolving times. When it comes to climate change and global warming, for instance, how will we respond to clients, particularly from the younger generation, who are petrified of the dangers to our planet and humanity? Take a look at this case study:

Case study: Yuri is coming for counselling with Jasmin. She begins the session by stating that she is anxious. Jasmin asks her what is going on for her, and she presents her issues as "relationship stress". She states that she hopes to learn useful tools in therapy to help her navigate this. Later in the session she says, in passing, that she had seen something on the news about climate change that day, and it had put her on edge. Jasmin, on hearing this, feels a slight pang of anxiety within herself. As it seems like just a passing comment, she doesn't feel she needs to attend to it, and her and Yuri move onto the formal issues as presented.

Analysis: Jasmin displays a seeming reluctance to explore Yuri's feelings around climate change further, and given her emotional response, we might wonder if Jasmin has ever thought about how she might find these types of conversations with clients? Of course, she could explore this in supervision, but if she herself is afraid of these issues, she might find this a challenge. Yuri's desired way of working is a more structured and technique-based approach, and we might be curious about the avoidance of what might be more existential types of conversation, by both parties. Might there be some merit, therefore, in bringing the topic back into the room in another session? Sometimes, for a client to make any sort of sense of something, they need their therapist to be bold, and show they are not afraid to walk by their side, in an authentic yet empathic way. This might mean, when therapeutically beneficial, taking a slight lead on something as a form of active acknowledgement. In this example, Jasmin would certainly not be pushing her own agenda on "green" issues, but instead would be reading between the lines, and responding to all of Yuri's needs in a permissive way.

The implications of private practitioners belonging to a minority cultural group

Some clients from minority cultures will be looking to choose a therapist who they feel might have a similar lived experience. At times this might be obvious to the client, such as by a therapist's skin colour, or by them seeking out specialised private services, for example, ones that work specifically with neurodivergent clients. But at other times our cultural lived experience may not be obvious. Therefore, when we think about how we market our practice, and how we present ourselves in other spaces, such as on social media, it's important to consider this. Ethically speaking, giving clients greater choice in terms of accessing a therapist with whom they might identify and feel more comfortable with, or who they believe may understand their experiences better, is a definite positive. Some private practitioners have chosen for this very reason to centre their entire practice around one type of client group, such as working with the LGBTQ+ community. But on the other hand, therapists ought to also be free to make their own decisions around if they wish to overtly reveal parts of their own culture. Although we advocate for authenticity from the private practitioner, how exactly each therapist might choose to do that is up to them. We rarely as human beings constantly reveal every single aspect of ourselves, in order to "qualify" as being authentic, so ethical practice could also mean the private practitioner *not* revealing aspects of their cultural identity, particularly if to do so would make them feel worried or insecure, or likely to have a negative effect on the work.

Sometimes therapists question the ethics around too much self-disclosure, wondering if revealing too much about our intersectional cultural identity leans towards making the space about us as opposed to focussing on our clients. As we touched on in Chapter 4 when discussing marketing our practices, as authors we are advocating for the notion of being professional, AND remaining as humans. For us, this means allowing the human within the therapist to exist. And that is different to pushing an agenda on our clients or taking up too much of the space. There is no set way to be a therapist, or a private practitioner – what's most important is reflecting on what we do, and why we do it, in line with our chosen ethical code.

Working with diversity: two examples

Case Study: Jacob, who identifies as a black, working class, heterosexual man, has come to therapy with Jason, for anxiety-related issues. One day he comes to his session and speaks about his experience of racism at work. Jason, who is white, middle-class, and heterosexual, listens and acknowledges that it "sounds difficult". He then says nothing further, and the conversation moves on.

Analysis: Jason's chosen intervention, although not technically incorrect, is lacking when we look at it from a culture lens. Jacob perhaps might have wanted more from Jason, a deep empathy which fully acknowledges his experience, and creates a space to talk further about it. Because what he has mentioned will no doubt extend beyond just this situation, to other situations he will have faced in his life, as a black man. Being with our client's side by side, unafraid to ask questions sensitively, and hearing and wanting to know about the pain that prejudice can bring, is part of ethical relational work. Showing that we truly want to understand the inner world of our clients, and we are not going to replicate the social structures that so often permeate it, by being too passive or too afraid to pry, for fear of saying the wrong thing. For when it comes to the unseen scars of discrimination and prejudice that are borne in the relational world, by doing nothing we are still actually doing something. As Delroy Hall (2021) asks aptly in his chapter in the book, *Black Identities + White Therapies*: can you talk about race without going pink or feeling uncomfortable?

Case Study: Jon has been in therapy with Kareem for a few weeks. In the session, they began to speak about his late teenage years, and Kareem noticed that Jon seemed to be avoiding talking about his past romantic relationships, or his experience of sex. Kareem had noticed that in the initial session, Jon had spoken about his "partner", but hadn't given a name, or many other details, and that in subsequent sessions, he refers to his partner using the pronouns "they". Finally, Kareem noted how Jon had told him the name of a local bar that he had been to the previous weekend, and it was a place Kareem knew to be an LGBTQ+ venue. Taking everything into account, Kareem suspects that Jon might identify as gay or bisexual, but he doesn't feel that it's his place to bring this up. He also wants to keep a non-judgemental stance, and avoid making any mistakes (in case he is wrong in his hypothesis).

Analysis: Although Kareem may be trying to be non-invasive and sensitive to Jon's reluctance to engage in or develop conversations around relationships, this might have the opposite effect. A lifetime of second guessing how people might react to a person being gay, and/or shame around sexuality, is likely to present within the therapy space too. In fact, Jon is gay, and did feel very unsure about how Kareem might respond. Kareem could balance remaining sensitive, empathic, and ever mindful of the other possibilities beyond his own assumptions (one being that the term "they", for instance, could have also suggested a non-binary or trans partner, as opposed to evasive language around the sex of his partner), with pushing just a little, to open the conversation up. In doing so, he could show a genuine curiosity from a

non-judgemental place – a kind of purposeful "anything you say is fine" atti-
tude. This might give more space to the possibility of Jon sharing more. The
shame that Jon is experiencing could become an opportunity for exploration,
as opposed to a block in the work, and a microcosmic repetition of what he
has experienced in his life. In the book *Queering Psychotherapy*, a conversation between editor Jane Czyzselka and author Robert Downes (2022, p. 47)
discusses the importance of naming shame in the therapy room, with Downes
stating: "so, in time I invite myself and my clients to breathe into shame, to
embrace it with the breath, to make room for the painful stories and realities
that usually unfold from shame."

Accessible practice

Another serious ethical consideration for private practitioners is paying attention to how accessible your practice is. As business owners, we have legal
responsibilities around making reasonable adjustments, in line with The
Equalities Act in 2010 (The UK Government, 2023), but also as therapists
we have an ethical duty to endeavour to create the most inclusive business
setting that we can. Some of this involves physical action that we need to take
as private practitioners when setting up our business, such as intentionally
making any general reasonable adjustments, whilst others focus more on our
communication with potential clients. For instance, a wheelchair user when
seeking therapy ought to be able to easily identify which therapists provide
a physical space which they can access, via clear details around accessibility
laid out in a private practitioner's marketing. If it is difficult for a private
practitioner to have made this reasonable adjustment, for instance, if they are
on the top floor of an old Victorian building (and they don't own the building), then this should also be very clear on their websites and directories. In
addition, it would be prudent for them to explore whether they can offer other
means of therapy for wheelchair users, such as online. Another crucial aspect
of communication is being able to engage in empathic, honest conversations
with potential or new clients around any adjustments they may need, and,
again, not being afraid to ask questions. So, if you have a new client who is
visually impaired, what is it they might need? It's important to have these
conversations both before starting the therapy, and when they arrive (Rattray,
2023). For the former, the client might need to request an adjustment to some
of your paperwork, such as the contract, by having it provided in large or
giant print. And when they arrive, they might, for example, ask you to meet

them at the front door and walk with them, providing instructions about the route to your consulting room. Always remember that not all disability or diversity is visible. Being open to this, and providing a generally inclusive environment will help create a comfortable and supportive experience for any client seeking therapy.

Part 2 – Money, money, money!

So, reader, how does this sub-heading make you feel?! Take a pause, and tune into any feelings that this word elicits in you. Money is a big word in private practice, and its significance cannot be ignored. Although we have touched on aspects of this in our chapter on contracting, there are many other ways in which money plays out in the room of a private practitioner. Raising our social awareness collectively as a profession also includes being tuned into the issues that a private practitioner might face themselves, and money is something that will not only be part of our "present", but also part of our whole life experience. The ethical considerations about how we work with money in the room, and the interactions that we have with our clients around this, are, therefore, not necessarily straightforward. Throw into this wider political issues around the nature of our work, and expectations around the private practitioner's role in contributing to larger societal needs, and we are faced with multi-layered challenges.

Catherine Jackson's 2023 article, "The big issue: Counting the cost", stated the various growing difficulties in the post-pandemic period, including a rise in people needing therapy and an economic crisis (known colloquially as "the cost-of-living crisis"), all at a time when statutory services were already struggling to cope (Jackson, 2023). Most private practitioners that we, the authors, know offer some form of sliding scale system, or have low-cost spaces in their practice. This is largely because the problems around fair accessibility to therapy are well-known. Therapists mostly do the job they do because they vehemently believe in the power of therapy, and therefore also believe in the principle that people ought to be able to access therapy, regardless of their economic status. But at the same time, expectations around us lowering our fees to meet demand – from both outside the sector and within – can be damaging for private practitioner's own lives and businesses. The truth is that private practitioners who do not charge enough are more likely to burn out, because they may need to see more clients just to be able to meet their own living needs. And burnt-out therapists are not only no good for our profession, but also create an unsafe situation for clients. The notion of "giving back" is, in theory, wonderful, as it represents the relational work we do, and how we care about clients, but it is, in practice, an unworkable one. Yes, some therapists will be able to offer a multitude of pro bono or low-cost slots, because of their own individual circumstances, but the idea that this needs to be a norm in the world of private practice is a threat to the sector. With the growing numbers of those working in private practice, to be truly socially aware as a profession, we need to be open to the varying economic circumstances of therapists, and make sure we are standing up for the protection of all, in an equitable way. The difficulties around access to therapy and the shortfall in statutory services is heart-breaking, but it cannot be rescued by private practitioners, many of whom, as we have already touched on, may have had to enter the private sector because paid employment was not so forthcoming.

There are workable ways for private practitioners to strike a good balance. First, standing up for yourselves, and pushing against binary notions, which stem from assumptions that we all occupy the same social standing in society. Second, by creating boundaries around low-cost places within our practice, such as having a set number of slots; having them at certain times of the day; creating a system of who qualifies for these places, which is clearly communicated on your website, and asking to be alerted by those looking for concessionary spots at the first point of call. Third, therapists can be active if they so wish, in helping such causes, through more indirect routes, away from their own practices, such as government lobbying.

The psychology of money – lowering fees: two case studies

> **Case Study A:** Phil has been working in private practice for eight months. He has been operating what he calls "a full private practice" and the feedback he receives from his supervisor is that he is progressing well as a therapist. He has a set number of clients that he likes to see in a week, and this number allows him to live comfortably. A client has recently ended, and he is eager to take on a new client, but when two weeks go by and he hasn't received an enquiry, he begins to panic that his business is faltering. He starts to change some of the wording on his website, hoping this will help, and when he sees his supervisor, informs her that he is considering lowering his fees – just in case.

Exercise
Do you think Phil's choices will help improve the situation? If you knew him as a friend, are there any other pieces of advice or words of support you would want to give to him?

Case Study B: Jenny has been working in private practice for three years. She started at the beginning of 2020, coinciding with the arrival of the Covid-19 pandemic. Her practice has taken off well, which she judges by the number of enquiries she receives, and her practice is full. This, despite having discussed with her supervisor the difficulties in predicting usual "trends" during the Covid period, such as which months year on year are busiest. Recently she has begun to notice, that the rate of enquiries has suddenly become much slower. Even though she doesn't have space to see anymore clients, she wonders what this means, and feels nervous.

Analysis: Returning to case study A, two weeks may seem like a relatively short amount of time for a private practitioner to begin to worry about their business falling apart, but it is a surprisingly common occurrence. Being self-employed creates all kinds of concerns, particularly if it is the therapist's only income. But we need to careful about muddying actuality and anxiety. We know as therapists ourselves that anxiety can create all kinds of behaviours, some of which are not necessarily useful, such as the desire to control. If we can feel that we can make changes as a means of dealing with uncertainty, or if we can blame ourselves by thinking it is because our marketing is not good enough, or we are not a good enough therapist, it can feel like we are doing something productive. Whilst there are certainly times where developing our practice is essential, the timings of this are crucial. Otherwise, the only thing we may be doing is playing into insecurity, and, in the process, knocking our confidence as practitioners. We can see this much more clearly in case study B, where Jenny is also beginning to worry, even though she doesn't need more clients! There is a direct correlation between what is an unknown and her anxiety about her practice. Psychologically, worry can be a difficult thing to sit with as a private practitioner. As with anyone though who is self-employed, there is always uncertainty, as it is part of the territory. Private practitioners can help themselves by being as prepared as they can financially, which means actively putting money aside each month; perhaps more at times when their practices are busier, to help with both the shock and the very real financial practicalities when quieter times arise. And there is benefit in embracing the uncertainty – being robust enough to "weather the storm" is a skill that a private practitioner arguably must learn. The two work together: if you know you can cover your rent for the next three months whatever happens, then you have more space to focus on grounding yourself and drawing your attention to your belief in you, and the practice you have built.

Setting your fees

It is generally expected that fees might be dictated by qualifications. This is evidenced by the fact that many counselling psychologists who have completed a first degree in psychology (or a conversion Masters), before their practical doctorate training, tend to charge more. But fees in private practice also rise with experience. A therapist who has nearly 10,000 clinical hours' worth of experience, although not necessarily "better", are, simply by virtue of their years of work, more likely to have seen a wider and diverse range of people and/or presenting issues. And this type of experience holds value. Therefore, a private practitioner will do well to have their fees reflect that fact. It's also good modelling, and part of community support, to make sure you're charging in accordance with your worth – remember new and upcoming private practitioners may be scouring the directories in their area to try and ascertain what they might charge. Seeing rates that adequately reflect, i) the average going rate for the area in which a therapist works, and ii) the slight differences between therapists, based on their knowledge/expertise, helps private practitioners set fees that are realistic and fair, to both themselves and clients, in addition to helping the sector hold its value.

For any private practitioner, reasonable, regular fee increases is a smart move for the longevity of your practice. Although there are no set rules, ethical thinking around *how* you do this is important. For example, some private practitioners will only feel comfortable raising their fees with new clients, whilst others believe it's fairer to keep all those who can pay on the same fee. If you do the latter of these options, it could be written clearly into your contract that fees will increase annually (and by how much). In fact, sometimes it is useful for private practitioners to do this, as it sets a boundary for themselves to stick to! Another option is to give existing clients plenty of notice, and enter into conversations with them individually. The benefits of this are that it allows for a more personalised way of communicating your plans in an intentional way, whilst also giving space for the clients to express any feelings they have about that. Relational ethical working means responding to the needs of each client as we see fit; being ever present in the therapeutic process, and mindful of balancing this with the needs of your business. Remember the reasons behind rising wages extend beyond experience, and a desire to earn more – if you are planning on a lifetime career in private practice, it just makes sense. Higher fees mean more wiggle room to lower the number of clients you see at any given time, which would be particularly important if you were nearing burn-out, going through a difficult time in your personal life, feeling more tired, wanting to change things up a bit in your practice, or just wanting to see less clients. This kind of flexible thinking and adaptability in your own practice is very important to an ongoing, ethical, thriving practice.

We mentioned earlier the importance of a private practitioner putting money aside, and this is also relevant when financially factoring into their schedule the times they are not working during the year (due to holidays/bank holidays etc.), as well as what we might refer to as "the slower months". The realities (and one of the downsides) of private practice is that there are slow months within the year. Although some of these trends have changed in recent years due to external factors such as the COVID-19 pandemic and the cost-of-living crisis, it is still understood that the height of summer will be a low time, because many people will be going on holiday, so are either not around or are less likely to spend money on therapy services. On the other hand, January is almost always likely to be a busier month, as people sometimes find the Christmas period hard, and come into the New Year with resolutions and plans, which may include working on their mental health. It is vital that a private practitioner can earn extra money in the months of the year where they are more likely to have clients coming through their practice, to substitute for when there may be less clients, and therefore less income. For all the practical reasons why this is important, the correlation between private practitioners being overly worried about income and compromise of ethical practice is a very real phenomenon (Binstead, 2022).

What is your money mind-set?

Ever heard the cliche about money being a dirty word?! Private practitioners sometimes feel a sense of guilt when it comes to money matters. And our own relationship with money can easily play out alongside a client's relationship with money. Have a look at the following case study:

Case study: Mai Ling has a new client, Jules. Jules is in full-time work and has been coming for counselling for six weeks. When Mai Ling conducts a review with Jules at this point, she states that she wishes to continue with the sessions but that she cannot afford the current fee, which is £60. She asks if she can continue on a reduced rate. This has caught Mai Ling unaware, and feeling rushed to make a decision, she agrees that Jules can instead pay £10 less. On reflection afterwards, she convinces herself that this was the right decision, because she didn't feel it was her place to prematurely end the counselling with Jules (who had been making steady progress). She also thought that perhaps her fee was a little high and lowering it for one client wouldn't do any harm. A couple of weeks later, Mai Ling couldn't help but notice that Jules had a new designer handbag which she thought looked quite expensive. A month later, it came up in conversation that Jules owned a second home, for which she received a rental income on top of her regular job. Mai Ling feels deceived by Jules and believes there was in fact no reasonable grounds for reducing her fee.

Points of reflection

- We might wonder what Mai Ling feels she is worth. She seemed very quick to decide to both reduce her fee and question if her regular fee is reasonable.
- Mai Ling seems to have taken what the client said at face-value, but she hasn't considered whether her understanding of not being able to afford something matches with Jules'.
- Has Mai Ling thought about how she handles clients that potentially push boundaries?
- Has Mai Ling looked at her own relationship with money? Has she ever discussed her experience of money, and or wealth/poverty throughout her own life, in a therapy space? Has she discussed in supervision how she finds working in a role where she is handling the money?
- Could she have held her boundary, whilst at the same time giving an empathic and open space to hear Jules' concerns about the fee?
- If Mai Ling was convinced that Jules did have valid current needs, might there have been a different approach that could have been taken? Perhaps one that reflected more of a carefully thought-out bending of her boundary,

even one that might produce a temporary solution, with clear parameters, rather than a quick fixed changing of her boundary.

- We might also want to also question how Mai Ling feels about on-the-spot decisions? Does she need to speak to her supervisor about how to better cope with ethical decisions when there are unexpected questions from clients?
- Mai Ling feels deceived. Might this now impact her work with Jules?
- Could Mai Ling have created an unconscious (or conscious), unspoken expectation for "something in return", i.e. for Jules to stay as her client long term in therapy, now the fee has been reduced.
- Is there anything else you might add? Can you discuss this example in your own supervision space, or with peers, to think more deeply about such scenarios?

TAKE-AWAY MESSAGES: As private practitioners we need to be ever mindful of the social, political, and cultural factors that will affect our clients, as well as ourselves. Private practitioners cannot escape money being "in the room", and it's important for us all to consider how this can affect both client and therapist, on an emotional and practical level. Don't forget the importance of working with cultural sensitivity, and how a continual process of education and self-exploration is crucial.

References

Binstead, C. (2022). *Negotiation of the business with ethical, therapeutic practice.* BACP. www.bacp.co.uk/bacp-divisions/bacp-private-practice/private-practice-tool kit/negotiation-of-the-business-with-ethical-therapeutic-practice/.

Downes, R. (2022). Queer shame: Notes on becoming an all-embracing mind. In Czyzselska, J. (Ed.), *Queering psychotherapy* (pp. 27–37). PCCS Books.

Hall, D. (2021). Can you talk about race without going pink or feeling uncomfortable? In Charura, D., Lago, C. (Eds.), *Black identities + white therapies* (pp. 43–64). Karnac.

Jackson, C. (2023). The big issue: Counting the cost. *Therapy Today*, 33(10). www. bacp.co.uk/bacp-journals/therapy-today/2022/december-2022/the-big-issue/

Rattray, S (2023). Good Practice in Action 129 *Reasonable adjustments in the counselling professions in private practice.* BACP. www.bacp.co.uk/media/18431/bacp-reasonable-adjustments-crp-gpia129-update-2023.pdf

Turner, D. (2023). Intersectionality, power and privilege. In Hanley, T., Winter, L. A. (Eds.), *The Sage handbook of counselling and psychotherapy* (pp. 30–33). Sage Publications.

The UK Government (2023). *Equality act 2010*. www.legislation.gov.uk/ukpga/2010/15/contents

Chapter 9

Managing endings in an ethical way

Caz Binstead and Nicholas Sarantakis

Grant me the serenity to accept the things I cannot change, the courage to change the things I can, and the wisdom to know the difference.

As the quote that opens this chapter implies, change can be an extremely complex and challenging thing for humans. The Serenity Prayer – with its exact origins unclear – is generally traced back to the theologian, Reinhold Niebuhr, but best known for its use within the AA Fellowship and 12-step programme (Alcoholics Anonymous, 2024; Sifton, 2011), where it promotes the wisdom of personal insight (DiGangi et al., 2014). Despite its relative simplicity, it holds profound meaning, and is something that one of the authors (Caz) regularly comes back to when thinking about therapy endings. The notions encapsulated – acceptance, courage, and grace – are – for both therapist and client – important themes when it comes to endings. Because endings are not *just* about the ending, but hold within them what has come before and what comes next. Clients embark on a courageous journey when they begin therapy, and having space at the end, to explore the path they have taken with graciousness and respect is a gift we give to them. In relational therapy, it is also one we give to ourselves. Planned endings that have been prepared for can be seen as transformational stepping stones, and are, according to Yalom (1975, p. 365): "an integral part of the process of therapy ... if properly understood and managed ... an important factor in the instigation of change". BACP (2023) describes how a client having a good ending with a therapist can be life changing. We might argue that a therapist might not necessarily be able to control whether a client experiences a wholly "good" ending, but that we can certainly endeavour helping them experience one; being aware of what the conditions might be to make it so and paying attention to this.

In Chapter 5 we looked at contracting, and for the private practitioner this is where endings can be first introduced. We've talked in this book about the

DOI: 10.4324/9781003435624-9

importance of being transparent with our clients about the process of therapy, and, specifically, what that looks like in our respective practices. We would need to mention if there were any fixed limits to the duration of the therapy, which might be relevant, for instance, if only working short term with clients. And ensure we advise clients of the need to conduct regular reviews in the work, where we can put a specific and deliberate focus on aspects such as the progression of the work, how your client finds the space, and so on. This is turn, can encourage discussions about ending, where relevant. For private practice, this is especially important, because we need to be extra mindful of the risk of our clients becoming dependent on us and factors that might lead to this, as seen in this case study.

Case Study: Pamela, who has been working in private practice for one and a half years, has been working with Sally for nine months. Although Sally seems to have worked through her original present-ing issue, there has been no mention of ending by either party. Sally appears to be happy continuing to come along, and although Pamela knows that, theoretically, she ought to be doing regular reviews with Sally, when she thinks about it, she pushes the thought away. There are no obvious issues, so surely she doesn't need to bring it up.

We're now going to add another line of information, and take us to one of those taboo places:

Pamela regularly worries about being self-employed, and hopes her pri-vate practice continues to thrive, so she can keep earning a living.

We don't know that this new information has any connection with Pamela's reasons for not doing a review with Sally, but it certainly is possible that it could be an additional factor, even if coming from an unconscious (or "out of awareness") place. Sometimes, if we're not reflecting on all levels within the context that we work, it can be easy to convince ourselves that taking a particular course of action is for the benefit of the client only, and as the case vignette states, "Sally appears happy to be continuing". But the truth is that we cannot know what the reality of Sally's experience is without engaging with her on her experience of the therapeutic process, in an open and rela-tional way.

Another aspect of the contract is sharing your expectations around ending. Of course, we cannot force our clients to do ending sessions with us, but it's useful at this point to mention your thoughts on them. You might state why you view ending sessions as an important part of the process, and what your hopes might be. Although the amount of ending sessions for each client will likely vary because there will be a big difference between a client who has come to therapy for four months and a client who has come for four years, stating the number of sessions that you would at least hope a client could commit to, has some merit. It is a good way of a) putting in some certainty (that might have some flexibility), to counteract an otherwise uncertain and unknown process, and b) being realistic about what a client might engage with, especially once they have decided to end. As we shall see, there are various emotional processes a person can go through when it comes to endings, and creating space for this is paramount. In fact, putting in a minimum amount of endings sessions as part of your practice boundaries, and thereby creating some structure, allows the potential for containment, safety, resolution, and celebration.

Navigating endings

Endings are synonymous with loss and change. What we desire for our clients is that there will be a hopefulness that comes with the decision to end – an excitement about the new, and an eagerness to turn the corner and start on a new path. As much as I (Caz) enjoy writing in a lovely philosophical way, the truth is that endings can be somewhat messier and more unpredictable than we might guess. When we make a change, and it is one that we have decided for ourselves, we often focus on the positives, which is understandable. But when you think about the ending of therapy, as the ending of a deeply meaningful process, we cannot help but be confronted with the ensuing losses. What parts of the client are being left behind in the space? How will the client make sense of the loss of the relationship they have with their therapist? What reaction will they have to the loss of ritual in attending? How do they make sense of the unpredictability of what it will be to not have their therapy space? Attending to such questions, and any other anxieties around what the loss of the space means, is paramount and helps affirm your client's experience. For clients who have previously experienced traumatic endings in their lives, this can be a powerful and fulfilling growth experience. Continuing to commit to being present to our client's experiences in an active way, until the absolute very end, is the ultimate respect to our clients, and the work. This includes the complexities that often come with endings. Murray Parkes (1996) argues when talking about loss that the unfamiliar and unpredictable can be frightening, and Bowlby spoke about the "cognitive biases" that can arise when faced with present-day losses which are influenced by our early attachment experiences (Humphrey & Zimpfer, 2008). Understanding our reactions to loss is to understand life, because we only know death through life, and vice versa. And so, exploring what the therapy space meant to our clients, as well as the ending itself, is paramount.

Endings in action

Case Study: Stephan has been working with Michelle in her private practice for two years. He has recently decided to end therapy, although he has mixed feelings. He feels like it's the right time and that he is in a much happier place, but he also wonders how he will maintain what he has achieved in the space, and if he will be able to continue to look after his mental health on his own. Michelle feels very proud of Stephan, and the work that they have done together, and welcomes him choosing to end. She verbalises her excitement for him, and feeds back to him on how far he has come, and how empowering it must be for him. She seems quite closed in her approach to the ending, and doesn't offer any further opportunity for discussion. Not wanting to disappoint Michelle, Stephan decides to hide his ambivalence. Afterall, he has enjoyed working with her and likes her a lot – he doesn't want to ruin what "should" be a celebration.

Analysis: Let's use our three-dimensional model to explore this further.

Client: Stephan has made the decision to end at what he believes is the right time, so in some ways what Michelle is saying to him could indeed be fair and true. However, the issue is not in what she is saying, but in her general approach to the ending. She isn't offering an opportunity to explore what is present in Stephan's experience, and gives the impression that anything other than celebratory is wrong. Stephan is stifled, along with his very valid concerns.

Therapist: We don't know what's going on for Michelle, but we might wonder how she responds to endings herself. Despite endings being such an important part of the therapy process, literature suggests that it can be challenging for therapists (Ling & Stathopoulou, 2020). It appears that she is gravitating towards pleasant emotions only, rather than being open to all of Stefan's possible feelings. This possible avoidance might tell us something about Michelle, which she would do well to explore further, as unresolved issues around endings, or simply a lack of awareness around how we generally relate to endings can have a direct impact on client work.

Societal: Western society does not generally embrace or encourage conversations around loss and endings, so culturally speaking, avoiding such conversations might make some sense. Stephan is also being very polite and is willing to hide his feelings to not make Michelle (his therapist) feel awkward. This resonates with a politeness that can often exist around grief in Western culture, where we might see a reticence to move more into emotion (our own, and others), and vocally express all that is there.

When it comes to ending sessions, being overt, detailed, and open about the date you are ending with a client, the number of ending sessions (including counting down as you go along, to remind the client of how long you have left), the utilisation of these sessions as you prepare for the ending, and the welcoming of your joint relational experience is always recommended.

Post-therapy considerations

Given the importance that we give to endings in therapy, we might assume that once we end with a client, that's it. And often it is. It can, in fact, be quite disconcerting at times to be a therapist and never know what has happened to the clients we have worked with; some of whom we have long-term relationships with. But this is the nature of our job, and keeping the boundaries around these endings, in a way which signifies a finality, is crucial. Sometimes, it's not final, but it's up to our clients only to decide if they wish to re-open a therapeutic relationship with us. Often private practitioners will indicate if a client can come back to the space should they wish to at any time, and this feels like a supportive approach. For the client who is nervous about ending, giving a brief and gentle reassurance that there is a secure base to return to if needed, without pressing the point too much, can be helpful in encouraging clients to take the leap into the fearful unknown. But not every private practitioner might be able to offer this, and ethically speaking, it is better to be clear with your client about whether this is realistic or not (for example, if your practice is always full, you may find fitting in returning clients harder). Private practitioners will do well to give this some real thought, as sometimes clients themselves will raise this question.

Premature endings

It is notable that on the BACP's "Endings – what complaints tell us" page (BACP, 2023), the first three points that clients have complained about their therapists for are all to do with premature endings instigated by the therapist:

- Ending their therapy abruptly, without notice or preparation.
- Ending by text or email, without offering a final session.
- Making the decision to end therapy on their own rather than by mutual agreement with the client.

There can be several reasons why a therapist may choose to end with a client. Often, it's because something difficult has come to the surface, and the private practitioner feels that ending the therapy might be the solution to the problem. As we can see from the complaints list though, this can really upset clients. It can cause feelings such as powerlessness and confusion … sometimes, a client feels rejected, or that they have failed in some way. It is often not about the clients themselves though. For instance, a private practitioner might end the work in an attempt to rectify their own mistakes, such as failing to say no to taking on a client who was outside of their competency level on, and then realising a little too far down the line (say, session 13). This kind of panic can unfortunately, often lead to premature endings in the private practice setting (Binstead, 2023). First off, therefore, is the recognition that thinking wisely about how the decisions we make in private practice might impact us in the long term as well as the short term is always likely to be beneficial. Practice saying no! And work in your supervision spaces to be clear on who you can work with, and also what types of presenting issues you *want* to work with. Otherwise, of course, we do not need the client's permission to end, and in our private practices, we must sometimes, with consultation, make decisions that we feel are for the best. Furthermore, it might be unavoidable, and the various reasons a private practitioner may end with clients range from moving out of the area in which they have been based, going on maternity leave, suffering burn-out, taking a sabbatical, and many more. Being empathic and doing what's best for our clients takes precedence, however. This includes giving as much notice as possible (and being mindful that longer-term clients might need notice that is proportionate to the time worked together), offering endings sessions, signposting to other support services (including potentially assisting with finding a new therapist), and giving space in the session for the client to air their feelings. Remember everything we said earlier about the meaning humans place on endings, often based on previous life experience? Sensitivity and attention to endings in such scenarios will go a long way.

Of course, sometimes clients choose to abruptly leave therapy themselves, and it's possible we may never know why, which understandably can bring up feelings of confusion or loss for the private practitioner. It's again part of our job to occasionally sit with the difficult feelings and unknowns. Different modalities may approach what's known as a DNA (did not attend) in varying ways, ranging from doing nothing (which represents respecting the client's autonomy and agency in making that decision, and the choice not to make contact), to sending a relational email, which might be "checking in", and inviting a client to attend an ending session, if they so wish. It's worth noting that in private practice however, this might be further complicated by cancellation agreements and potential unpaid fees, as well as, where relevant, a lack of clarity about whether to continue holding a set slot for the client. Some of this, particularly regarding the latter point, could be pre-addressed in your contract, with wording such as "in the eventuality that …". Otherwise, if a client has decided to end, collecting any outstanding payments will become purely a business transaction, and it would be wise to view it as separate to any further therapeutic intervention.

Take a moment now to connect with yourself, and tune into how the ending of this chapter makes you feel. Sometimes … it's just not the way we want it.

> *TAKE-AWAY MESSAGES: Ensuring that those we work with can have a "good enough" ending is the commitment we give to our clients. Unknowns can be difficult for client and therapist alike, but embracing a congruent position, shrouded in ethical practice, will help the private practice navigate endings.*

References

Alcoholics Anonymous (2024). *Literature listings.* A.A World Services. www.aa.org/origin-serenity-prayer-brief-summary

BACP (2023). *Endings: What complaints tell us.* BACP. www.bacp.co.uk/about-us/protecting-the-public/professional-conduct/what-complaints-tell-us/endings/

Binstead, C. (2023). *Supervision for those new to private practice: An essential element to setting up ethical and thriving practice.* [Workshop session] Onlinevents. https://onlinevents.co.uk/courses/supervision-for-those-new-to-private-practice-caz-binstead/

DiGangi, J., Majer, J., Mendoza, L., Droege, J., Jason, L., Contreras, R. (2014). What promotes wisdom in 12-step recovery? *Journal of Groups in Addiction and Recovery*, 9(1): 31–39. www.ncbi.nlm.nih.gov/pmc/articles/PMC4051299/. doi: 10.1080/1556035X.2013.836869

Humphrey, G., Zimpfer, D. (2008). *Counselling for grief and bereavement* (2nd edn.). SAGE.

Ling, L., Stathopoulou, C. H. (2020). An exploration of ending psychotherapy: The experiences of volunteer counsellors. *Counselling and Psychotherapy Research*, 21(3), 729–738. doi.org/10.1002/capr.12379

Murray Parkes, C. (1996). *Bereavement: Studies of grief in adult life.* Penguin.

Sifton, E. (2011). *The serenity prayer – Faith and politics in times of peace and war.* W. W Norton.

Yalom, I. D., Leszcz, M. (1975). *The theory & practice of group psychotherapy.* Basic Books.

Chapter 10

Use of individual supervision vs. alternative supportive spaces

Caz Binstead and Nicholas Sarantakis

Supervision, described by Hawkins and Shohet (2012), is a

> joint endeavour in which a practitioner with the help of a supervisor, attends to their clients, themselves as part of their client practitioner relationships and the wider systemic context, and by doing so improves the quality of their work, transforms their client relationships, continuously develops themselves, their practice and the wider profession.
>
> (p. 60)

It is recommended for therapy professionals in the UK, by most of the professional bodies (NCPS, 2023; BACP, 2018). And, when it comes to private practice, it is paramount. If we acknowledge that private practice is a niche sector, then it equally makes sense for this to be respected within the supervision space. One of the authors Caz, argued in "The buck stops with you", that when it comes to choosing a supervisor: "it is particularly beneficial to have someone who understands all the different elements that make up a private practice, which include the business side such as practice management and marketing, and, how this fits alongside the ethical clinical work" (Binstead, 2022); an idea she later developed even further, by arguing the need for "specialist" private practice supervisors, particularly for those who are new to the private practice sector. She argues that among other things, the supervision space is crucial to exploring arising ethical dilemmas: "your supervisor really does have the potential to be your ace card, given the likely isolation of therapists in private practice and the levels of responsibility involved in running a private therapy practice" (Binstead, C, as cited in Lee & Sanders, 2022). In other words, your supervisor can fulfil some of the missing roles that you would ordinarily have, when working in other settings as a therapist,

DOI: 10.4324/9781003435624-10

as well as being a place to navigate mitigating isolation in other ways. Caz also argues, though, that a supervisor who doesn't know experientially about all the different elements involved in private practice, and the day-to-day experience of building a practice, may in fact lead to a supervisee feeling more isolated (Seabrook & Binstead, 2023). Hence, why private practice specialist supervision is so crucial.

Caz has advocated the benefits of using the Inskipp and Proctor model (Inskipp & Proctor, 1993) in the supervision space with private practitioners as a vehicle for the ongoing practice of deep reflexivity (which is taking place inside and outside supervision). Originally designed to describe the functions of supervision, Caz has adapted this model to fit with private practitioners specifically, with the idea first presented at the International Supervision Week 2022 (Binstead, 2023a). It is described here:

Formative (educative) relates to supervisees learning skills, development, and professional identity

Private practitioners develop at a rapid rate and are essentially learning on the job. A supervisor can help a private practitioner to not only develop as a therapist, but also specifically, as a therapist within the context of the setting in which they are working (private practice). They can also help with identifying what additional skills the supervisee may need to learn. Full supervision sessions might be devoted to learning skills which would be essential for ethical and safe practice, such as how the supervisee relates to, and conducts risk-assessments.

Normative (managerial) refers to accountability, developing best practice principles, ethical and legal considerations, compliance with organisational procedures and professional standards for the well-being of clients.

Private practitioners work on their own, and produce their own policies and procedures, therefore, the supervision space creates a chance to discuss and develop these, with the guidance of another party. An example might be the supervisee taking their contract along to the supervision space and running through it. Those who are new to private practice, may be developing their ethical decision-making, which is described in a concise way by Jo Langston, BACP's previous ethics services manager as: "the glue between the ethical framework and your practice" (Lees-Oakes & Kelly, 2023). This gives a chance for supervisors to check in with supervisees on how regularly they are engaging with their ethical framework. Best practice considerations might be focused on how a private practitioner balances the business side with the therapeutic work, such as how many clients a supervisee is seeing in a week, and how they might increase ethically, if/when, they want to. This is an example of an area that might be a particular challenge for the new private practitioner (and therefore also the supervisor), who may feel a conflict between what might be considered a sensible rate of gradual increase, and the need to earn a certain amount of money (to say, pay their rent or mortgage).

*Restorative (supportive) considers the impact of the work on the supervisee and the necessary psychological support and scaffolding required to "hold" the supervisee. This function can help mitigate the stresses and impacts of the work and promote practitioner well-being.

Private practitioners, as with all therapists, need to find ways to self-care. But the need is even greater for those who are working on their own in an isolated setting. A supervisor can offer ongoing support within the supervision space, and help a private practitioner factor self-care into their business plan.

The benefits of using this model are that it allows a flexible way of thinking about ethics, with regards to client work, your unique practice, yourself, and the profession. It provides an extra, crucial pair of eyes, which can help with noticing the aforementioned conflicts. This is especially pertinent if there is a block in thinking, particularly concerning elements of "the business" which the practitioner might be, for a variety of reasons, reluctant to talk about. Or if there are other factors at play, such as an ethical conflict between the needs of client and therapist, that has yet to be reflected on. It also encourages an appropriate level of humility for the private practitioner – to use their supervision space fully, in acknowledgement of that which is lacking in private practice (the scaffolding structure as discussed), while simultaneously not downplaying the importance of the independent levels of reflection that a private practitioner engages in. This process can be helped by finding a supervisor who brings an element of safety (whatever that means for you) … someone you envisage building a trusting relationship with, that will allow you to explore your work in an open and honest way.

Speaking the unspeakable in supervision

A plus side of private practice is being a self-employed professional, which means being able to work your own hours, and choose how many clients to have in your practice. But conversely for therapists, it can also be a downside. How tempting it may be to take on more clients, when you need a bit more money, or even when you feel bored! Yes, it's true – sometimes the isolation of private practice itself can cause therapists to bury themselves in the work. If we are beginning to get run down, feeling the effects of loneliness, or the stress of not being able to easily unburden, we need to be particularly careful. It can be surprisingly tempting to find unhealthy, distracting ways of dealing with this, which includes simply "upping" our client-load. It is important to feel you can talk about this stuff in supervision, because sometimes in the therapy profession, it feels taboo to admit such things, for fear of being called "unethical". Yet, we know that these are some of the unfortunate realities of private practice. And with a lack of support for private practitioners, many will not realise the importance of reflecting on these things until it is too late. A lack of support, and fear of professional shame can easily help create a vicious cycle, which in fact is more likely to cause unethical practice.

As private practitioners, we need to be kind to ourselves, and remember how we don't have access to some of the nurturing things that other therapists do, like those working in an agency. Simple things that many will take for granted, such as going into kitchen and seeing colleagues in your break, and the sheer appreciation of human contact (with people other than your clients), dropping in and touching base with a workplace manager if you need help with an ethical issue, or being able to engage with confidential peer support, to offload more easily. Of course, on the latter point, it is possible for private practitioners to access peer spaces; something we explore in this chapter (and later, in our chapter on social media), but that does require more time, thought, and space to do so, as opposed to it being on-sight in an agency or workplace. Reviewing the impact of lone working in your individual supervision space is an important part of looking after yourself as a private practitioner. There could well be more discussions around this when you are new to private practice, as you accommodate and settle into the sector, but it needs to be an ongoing process. Factors such as changes in our personal circumstances; changes to the field of private practice itself; and the possibility of complacency by those who have been working in private practice for some years, all need to be taken seriously.

Supervisors and private practitioners working together: the nurturing of the stable private practitioner

As discussed in Chapter 2, many new private practitioners tend to think a lot at the beginning of their journey, about how to quickly create a successful practice. But the wise mind will also keep one eye on factors that will increase the longevity of your private practice. Because for some people, this will be a life-long career. It's worth remembering, that you don't have an extra tool to do therapy, or to run your practice – YOU are the tool (Binstead, 2023a). Therefore, the stability of the practitioner themselves must always be in the foreground. The word "stable" is deliberate. We are not talking about "strong" or "robust", but, instead, a person who looks after themselves in the short term and the long term; acting with a degree of flexibility that enables them to remain in grounded control of themselves and your business. This case study shows how a supervisor and private practitioner can work together, to protect and nurture the private practitioner:

Case study: Patty has been working for six years as a private practitioner. Since beginning her practice, she has prided herself on having what she deems a successful practice. Many of her contemporaries know how dedicated she is to her private practice, and she is looked up to by others, particularly in social media circles, for her ideas about what makes a practice work. Then suddenly out of the blue, she begins to struggle to focus, and notices that she finds it more difficult to sleep. She keeps thinking that it is the insomnia she is experiencing that is affecting her day-to-day abilities, and this is why there never seems to be enough hours in the day to get what she needs done. In response she starts to work harder, ploughing herself into "doing"-type activities, while, simultaneously, being aware of her struggles with completing tasks of importance, or remaining present with clients. She's begun to notice that she is "clock-watching" a lot more, and sometimes finds being empathic a lot harder, which then, in turn, creates a spiral of self-criticism and anxiety. She begins to contemplate the possibility that she might be on the way to burn-out, and yet is resistant to take any action, such as telling her supervisor or dipping down on her clients.

She knows that if she does not address the issue, she may face the reality of not being able to work at all, and yet feels sad to potentially lose her constantly fully booked business by lowering her weekly client numbers. There are other losses too, including her identity as a well-known private practitioner with a successful practice.

Burn-out is defined as: "the injurious effects of stress particularly related to work" (Sutton & Stewart, 2008, p. 193). It can affect anyone, especially those in a helping profession, and as therapists, the levels of empathy that we give out constantly, and the amount of emotional "stuff" that we carry, can make it likely that, especially after many years of this work, we may suffer burn-out. The debilitating effects of burn-out cannot be underestimated, nor can the probability of private practitioners being more susceptible to it. It is much harder for private practitioners to take time off because they are self-employed and therefore do not receive sick pay, unless they have been paying into an insurance scheme which would cover such eventualities. Many private practitioners who begin to feel what they think might be the effects of burn-out, will have similar worries to Patty, in addition to concerns around money. The supervisor of the private practitioner needs to be very aware of factors that could prevent honesty around this within the supervision space. Shame might be a big one, as well as a fear of being boxed into a joint decision that they may then regret. This is where a private practitioner's potential defensiveness and protection around their practice could spike. Let's use our three-dimensional model to look at this:

Client: It is potentially dangerous for a therapist with burn-out to be working with vulnerable people. We know, for example, that therapists with burn-out can begin to behave in ways which indicates their suffering, such as ending sessions early, having a deficit of empathy, or less patience (due to irritation). Also, should the therapist completely burn-out, it might then mean a sudden and premature end to the work, which could be difficult for clients.

Therapist: Also, dangerous. For them to continue working at the same pace could put them out of action completely, not only causing serious health worries, but also disrupting their private practice completely, to the point where they cannot continue with it.

Societal: If a therapist is trying to ignore something as serious as burn-out, and not tending to self-care, what message does that send about our profession as a whole? On the other hand, how might the social positioning of the therapist as an individual be playing out here? If, say, someone is single and has worked hard and made their way through poverty and a working-class background, to set up a successful private practice on which their entire life income is based, how does the profession, of which supervisors represent (as a conduit between membership bodies and therapists), compassionately assist?

As we decipher the information drawn out in this model, it seems obvious that it would be very detrimental for the therapist to take no action. However, what this action looks like might be a gentle and balanced approach. The starting point would be for a supervisor to be eagle-eyed, and in tune with the private practitioner, meaning they are able to notice when something is amiss, that is, if the person presents as more tired, or they are making more mistakes in their work. They may even be communicating that they cannot sleep or are waking up early with anxiety. A supervisor who has good knowledge of this sector might observe the therapist's habits changing, such as their ability to keep up with the admin work of private practice. A good working symbiotic relationship between supervisor and private practitioner might lead to organic conversations about how the therapist is doing, and onto subjects such as burn-out. The language used doesn't have to be "burn-out" of course, but could just be something akin to it, that diffuses any shame, and instead focusses on a pragmatic way forward. A gentle and balanced approach as described above need not necessarily be a supervisor instructing you to stop work for everyone's benefit. If the issue is addressed before it hits crisis point, there are many ways to manage it, which might include:

- The therapist taking some holiday.
- The scheduling of a few odd days off over the coming months, to give some more free time for rest.
- A joint curiosity around the therapist's work/life balance. Is there, in general, enough self-care, downtime, fun time, and rest? Is there too much "therapy-related" stuff, and if so, could something else give?
- Talking about the possibility of the private practitioner entering into therapy themselves (if they are not already).
- Being curious together, about how much time the therapist spends on activities that could be detrimental to their health, and worsen burn-out. This could even include phone or social media usage. Can there be limits

put around such things to allow the brain to rest more, and to seek happiness instead, from (potentially) less dopamine inducing activities?

- Gradually dipping down on clients, by not taking on new clients when the old ones leave. This can be a temporary arrangement, and although a private practitioner may have various concerns about this, including financial implications, putting such steps in can allow recovery and healing, by helping prevent full burn-out. This might ultimately lead to a potential loss of the entire practice.
- Being mindful of how easy it can be to take on more enquiries as a private practitioner, and exploring together, *how* this is for the therapist in question. Working on being able to say no to new clients, even it feels tempting to take them on.
- Changing the work pattern around. Does the therapist need one afternoon off completely? If so, how can they work to ethically shift existing clients around, if needed?
- Is the private practitioner a supervisor as well? Is it possible to pause any supervision work? Especially given this role involves the tricky "holding" of many people.
- Seeing how nurturing activities can be worked into the therapist's schedule. Although it may seem like doing more things, in fact healthier types of things – suitable for the person in question – can have a positive effect.
- Seeing if the therapist can speak to their GP about their difficulties sleeping.
- Looking at the clients the therapist has. Being curious together about if there any clients in their practice, who might require a referral to someone else, for the benefit of both therapist and client. Careful and ethical referrals require consideration between supervisor and practitioner, but it's worth noting that sometimes there is no other option. Therapists sometimes feel like they need to martyr themselves, but it's important to remember that this is no good if that means behaving unethically on a broader level (such as ignoring situations that may be worsening burn-out).

Alternative supportive spaces: therapy

One of the items on the list to prevent burn-out is for the therapist to consider going into therapy themselves. This is of course what we might refer to as an "alternative supportive" space, vis-à-vis, our chapter heading. And for the private practitioner, this might be one of the best investments that can be made. Self-care is not just a buzz word, but a deeply important gift we give to ourselves, and an inward care, that feels respectful and honouring. And when it comes to a therapist's private practice, therapy might be an essential way of keeping the most important tool in the business in good shape. In terms of client work, we have an ethical commitment to be aware of relating to our own physical and psychological health, with the BACP "Ethical Framework for the Counselling Professionals" suggesting under Good Practice, point 91 (c) that practitioners are: "seeking professional support and services as the need arises" (BACP, 2018). It may be debated that this is an expense that some therapists cannot afford, and that they should feel free to make that choice as and when they see fit. It could also be argued that entering into therapy – including for therapists themselves – is a deeply personal decision, and that someone being in therapy simply because their supervisor advises them to would not be effective. On the other hand, the authors in this chapter have laid out some of the associated risks that comes with the isolated nature of private practice, and it would seem prudent for any therapist to properly consider this. The Ethics section in the BACP Framework states a selection of "Principles" that direct attention to a therapist's ethical responsibilities, and these include "Self-respect: fostering the practitioner's self-knowledge, integrity and care for self"; and "Being trustworthy: honouring the trust placed in the practitioner" (BACP, 2018). The latter point was highlighted by Caz in her workshop entitled *An Isolated Sector: Thinking about Holistic Self-Care in Private Practice* (Binstead, 2023b) where she talked with passion about taking seriously, the trust that clients put in us, and how we must endeavour to honour that as best we can, which includes taking our own self-care seriously. From a supervisor's perspective, it's not necessarily easy to navigate these types of conversations, especially if the supervisee is unaware of the potential need or is reluctant to go into therapy, but finding a way to guide the private practitioner into the reasons why this might be useful feels an important part of the role. One of the most important components of relational work is for the therapist to encompass the ability to understand and relate to the client as a living, breathing human being, who knows life – in all its bliss and pain. This means that it's vital that we as therapists can know when *we* need the support of a therapy space ourselves. You could argue that vehemently believing in therapy is an ethical stance because there is a level of congruence and authenticity that is happening on an unspoken level between client and therapist – a kind of:

> I know what it's like, the uncertainties, and the difficulties of life. The holes in our hearts that we sometimes experience, and I too, will honour our space, by respecting the power of therapy, and its existence. I too, am unafraid to find my own space when I most need it.

The pandemic was a whole new experience for therapists, and like our clients we faced difficult circumstances (Adams, 2023), which were hard to fully comprehend, and make sense of. One of the authors recently attended a concert at the London Palladium with the musical artist, Bonnie Raitt. Raitt, who at the time of the event, was aged 73, spoke candidly about death in-between the songs. She talked about musicians who were dear to her, being lost to Covid, and dedicated songs to their memory. She also talked about the temporary loss of live music owing to the various worldwide pandemic restrictions, when COVID-19 was at its peak. Her openness spoke of a truth that so many of us dare not speak. To connect with so many losses on so many levels, takes a certain kind of courage. Perhaps there was something about the quietness in-between the songs, coupled with the talk of loss and death, in comparison to her roaring guitar and music; so easy to get lost in, that brought home the difference between living free and unabated, and the experience of the diminishing of life in various ways. Yet therapists largely carried on during the pandemic times; all the while carrying our own responses to the pandemic, and that of our friends and family, as well as clients, and the ripples felt in the therapy room, from the client's friends, and families too. Although therapists do not count as key workers, the commitment that they have shown throughout the pandemic years has been one to be commended. Like others, the profession largely takes the view that it is a job, and you get on with it. But again, if we think about therapists as human beings, the need to reflect on the impact of our jobs, alongside our own lives, feels paramount. Private practitioners cannot underestimate the exhaustion that they will have, at times, been hit with. So, circling back around to conversations about therapists being in therapy seems fitting. Why not occupy a bit of realness "Bonnie Raitt" style, and truly take on the task of becoming a courageous client who is willing to explore the depths of our own experiences, and the after-effects of this once in a lifetime crisis.

Other supportive spaces: peer supervision groups and peer support

There are arguments to suggest that that an individual supervisor does not necessarily have a more credible guidance or professional opinion to offer to the private practitioner than that of their peers. Hence, we believe that peer supervision (within a group, or one-to-one context), where peers share their input and reflections about the clinical work with each other, can have equal value. In fact, the power balance between peers can be more empowering than that of an individual supervisor and supervisee (where there is certainly a power imbalance in favour of the supervisor), and can potentially help some people feel more open to exploring challenging areas of their practice. In addition, a peer supervision group can offer an array of perspectives from all members involved.

One of the authors, Nicholas, has an ongoing and rewarding experience of participating in peer-led, reflective supervision groups for years, as well as participating in peer-led residential group work between private therapists, which offers an alternative avenue of personal support to the practitioners. These types of spaces, which allow multiple perspectives from private practitioners, can be invaluable for helping the therapist manage common recurring things that come up. We have been reflecting in this chapter on self-care, and one of the best ways a private practitioner can pay attention to themselves is in the "in-betweens". By this we mean in-between sessions, and in-between the days, that we work with clients. Regarding the former, rituals and ways of being can be of great use to therapists. The work we do can be heavy, and hearing from other private partitioners on how they ground themselves and keep focussed during this time between clients can be enlightening and enriching.

Case study: Jake is regularly feeling tired at the end of his working day and finds that he has not been feeling as present at his work of late. He is discussing this in his peer supervision group, and one of the group members, Charlie, is keen to know what Jake does in the space between his clients (particularly, being aware that Jake sees up to six clients on some working days). Jake says that he never really thought that much about it, and he tends to just keep sitting so he can rest, but also mentions that, sometimes, he might go on his phone and check social media. The group discuss this, and it's mentioned by some members, that sitting without moving can make them at times feel stifled, and that it felt good to add some moving energy by getting out of their chairs. Some said they just needed to get up and walk, with others stating very specific things, such as walking over to the window, opening it, and leaning out, or walking around, throwing a small ball as a way to keep energised and focussed. It was generally agreed by the group that experimenting and finding out what worked for each individual felt important, and that honouring the therapist's separate being as a human in-between seeing clients was a good thing to do. The learning objective that came for Jake out of the conversation was to reflect on how he had been zoning out in these moments, and that he might do well to explore more what he might need in those moments, and to give attention to it.

Regarding "in-between" client days, it's worth remembering that a private practitioner might feel affected by something that has been heard in the work. There could be a lot of thinking and feeling in relation to it, and potentially also physical sensations such as headaches. Furthermore, it might not always be clear *why* we are experiencing certain thoughts, feelings, or bodily sensations, and of course that is something that can be discussed in a supervision space; particularly if we work with transference and countertransference (as it could be telling us something about a client and the therapeutic process). But in terms of looking after oneself, chatting with other private practitioners who are also holding their clients, and experiencing the potential pressures of running their own practice, can be hugely reassuring, and de-stigmatising. It could be suggestions of acknowledgement of the toll of holding heavy emotions: "I've been touched by some material today, and I accept in a loving way toward myself, that it is painful"; "I wonder if something has been stirred in me, that brings up some past wounds. How can I explore this more in a kind and compassionate way?" Or "wow, I'm really feeling anxious, and experiencing it as shoulder tension, which is unlike me. I might be learning something about a client, but can I for now, just care for myself and then discuss in detail in my next supervision". The group might also be able to suggest ways to self-care as a way of re-focussing, such as swimming; music; having a shower; meditation; running; changing clothes; cuddling pets/family members, and so on. Sometimes in the lived experience of isolation in the life of a private practitioner, we can easily lose ourselves, and start to believe that everything we think and feel is directly related to our life. However, our work is deep and powerful, and our response can be full of multi-layered meaning.

Of course, all the above observations do not intend to undermine the value of the traditional one-to-one supervision (or personal therapy) as sources of clinical and personal support for the private practitioners, but rather to highlight that there can be other, equally valuable, forms of support which can be available to the frequently isolated private practitioner. It does not have to be an either/or, but, rather, that we can use the type of support that would better respond to our needs at certain times.

TAKE-AWAY MESSAGES: A private practitioner can benefit from as many supportive spaces as possible. The isolation in this sector cannot be underestimated, and the key to longevity and happiness in your practice is knowing that there are various people and support systems to draw on. These spaces bring different benefits, so don't forget to lean into them, and allow yourself to be supported.

References

Adams, M. (2023). *The myth of the untroubled therapist: Private life, professional practice.* Routledge.

BACP (2018). *Ethical framework for the counselling professions.* BACP. www.bacp.co.uk/media/3103/bacp-ethical-framework-for-the-counselling-professions-2018.pdf

Binstead, C. (2022). *The buck stops with you.* BACP. www.bacp.co.uk/bacp-divisions/bacp-private-practice/private-practice-toolkit/the-buck-stops-with-you/

Binstead, C. (2023a). *Supervision for those new to private practice: An essential element to setting up ethical and thriving practice.* [Workshop Session]. Onlinevents. https://onlinevents.co.uk/courses/supervision-for-those-new-to-private-practice-caz-binstead/

Binstead, C. (2023b). *An isolated sector: Thinking about holistic self-care in private practice.* [Workshop Session]. Onlinevents. https://onlinevents.co.uk/courses/an-isolated-sector-thinking-about-holistic-self-care-in-private-practice-workshop-with-caz-binstead/

Hawkins, P., Shohet, R. (2012). *Supervision in the helping professions.* McGraw Hill Open University Press.

Inskipp, F., Proctor, B. (1993). *Making the most of supervision: A professional development resource for counsellors, supervisors and trainees.* Twickenham Cascade.

Lee, D. A., Sanders, P. (2022). *Step in to study counselling & psychotherapy* (4th edn). PCCS Books.

Lees-Oakes, R., Kelly, K. (2023). *BACP special: Starting a private practice in counselling.* Counselling Tutor. https://counsellingtutor.com/starting-a-private-practice-in-counselling/

NCPS (2023). *Code of ethical practice*. NCPS. https://nationalcounsellingsociety.org/assets/uploads/docs/National-Counselling-Society-Code-of-Ethics.pdf

Seabrook, M. (Host), Binstead, C. (Guest) (2023*). Caz Binstead – Private practice supervision. The craft of supervision podcast*. Spotify. https://open.spotify.com/episode/1umItO2gBGVMicziofBLGD

Sutton, J., Stewart, W. (2008). *Learning to counsel*. How To Books.

Chapter 11

Social media communities

A space to be heard?

Caz Binstead and Nicholas Sarantakis

Contemporary private practice means moving with the times and embracing new ways. Technology is a big part of this, and the rise in use of social media by therapists in general, but particularly private practitioners, has been exponential. Social media platforms open whole new ways to connect private practitioners across the country – even across the world! Given what we have already explored in terms of the impact of isolation on private practitioners, it is perhaps unsurprising that the combination of what is a seemingly natural inclination within modern society towards technology and the advent of the COVID-19 pandemic have led to an increase of online communities between therapists.

Private practice and social media

Social media is a place to convene with other therapists in a way which is relatively easy and time efficient. Private practitioners will be known to "pop on" in their working day, and for some it is a place where much time is spent. Isolation becomes a multi-layered phenomenon when considering the reasons that private practitioners may use social media. We have already somewhat discussed the literal physical isolation, as well as the isolation that comes with lone working and running a sole person business, but we also need to include here the collective of private practitioners as a visible entity within the therapy profession. Social media provides a space for working therapists in the counselling professions to be seen and heard, and as a free-to-access space, which is available to 24/7, it brings inclusivity to our profession in a way not seen before. Private practitioners also use the social media domain to grow their practices through a variety of ways and means. We hope you get some sense of how this can be done through our discussions in this chapter with some private practitioners.

DOI: 10.4324/9781003435624-11

Recent papers and resources on social media use by therapists

White and Hanley (2023), who wrote a paper on ethical dilemmas by therapists using social media, point out the discrepancies between the ethical guidelines from English-speaking countries, and suggest that providing guidance on this area was a difficult area to navigate. As a secondary study, they reviewed prior research, and came up with three useful recommendations – that social media is included in CPD (continuing professional development) and professional training, that there is continued reflexivity from the therapist, and that guidelines are: "dynamic and regularly updated" (White & Hanley, 2023). It's noted, however, that most studies they reviewed were from pre-pandemic times, and there is clearly room for more up-to-date literature.

A podcast chat between the two co-leads of the online #TherapistsConnect community – although not specific to private practitioners – provided a glimpse into the life of a working online therapy community. Caz Binstead and Dr Peter Blundell speaking at the beginning of 2023, about three years of running a therapist's social media community, observed that there was still generally a desire to talk about therapy, and share opinion and ideas about practice, as well form connections, despite ongoing changes in how therapists interacted with each of the unique social media platforms. They reflected on how one of the blessings was being able to connect with therapists worldwide, and discover more about the similarities and differences in working in different countries. And they acknowledged that there was a lot to be continually learnt about therapy social media communities, and the ways therapists use them (Blundell & Binstead, 2023). Private practitioners may feel relieved to hear that this territory, with all its positives, still feels relatively new and uncertain, even to those most immersed in it!

Ethical dilemmas

Here are a couple of ethical dilemmas based around social media use by a private practitioner. View the associated exercises and see if you can reflect further on these dilemmas, either on your own, in supervision, or as part of a peer group.

Case Study A: Jaap has been working on a weekly basis with Peter for two years, and considers them to have a good therapeutic relationship. One day, out of the blue Peter sends a friend request to Jaap on Facebook. Jaap feels anxious about this and is unsure on how to proceed. His initial reaction is that it is not appropriate, but he does not want to hurt Peter, or harm the relationship.

Exercise: What are the ethical considerations here? What might Jaap do (or not do)?

Case Study B: Cath has been a therapist for 15 years, and having spent much time in online therapist communities, feels relatively at ease with how she operates. She generally works with clients on a long-term basis, and believes that authenticity is a key part of what makes relational therapy effective. She is dedicated to ethical practice; frequently uses her supervision space to talk about ethical dilemmas, and has a digital policy in place. Cath is a music fan, and although does not speak about this explicitly with clients, feels in her heart that through both her general attire within the room and the possible occasional sight of her headphones sitting in her open bag, some clients may guess this. As such, she routinely shares music videos on her social media account. One day she is in a rush, and hears a song on the radio. Happily singing along, she shares another song by the same artist on her X/Twitter account without really thinking. In her next session with Mary, she senses some tension in the room and that Mary seems "off" with her. Trying her best to work with Mary in a relational way, hoping she will feel free to speak her mind, Mary eventually says how upset she was at the fact that she had stumbled on the post. She was shocked that Cath was sharing music by someone who in her mind is controversial. The artist had stood trial for a sexual abuse case, and although found not guilty, continued to have rumours swirling around them. Much of Cath and Mary's work was centred on Mary experiencing childhood sexual abuse, and she felt hurt that Cath had seemingly not considered this.

Exercise: What do you think of this case study? Does it evoke any strong feelings in you? How do you make sense of self-disclosure in the arena of social media?

Case example of a private practitioner using social media

John-Paul Davies mainly uses three social media platforms – X/Twitter, Instagram, and YouTube. He states that being on social media is largely a positive experience, as it allows him to find his voice, and gives him visibility. It has also acquired him a lot of clients from the USA, who have largely come via his YouTube channel. This is a social media platform that does not get talked about in therapist circles so much, and yet John-Paul swears by it. He cites the benefits as having adequate space to create more meaningful and authentic videos, which creates not only better content that people can connect with, but also a feeling of safety. John-Paul feels that prospective clients can get a better judge of who he is, and senses that this makes people feel more comfortable in approaching him for therapy. He points out that this space and freedom also means there is less likelihood of misinterpretation, as opposed to a platform like X/Twitter, where limitations such as how many characters can be used in a tweet can cause issues. He admits that there are some inevitable uncertainties that come with social media posting. For instance, you don't know, and will never find out, what potential clients might be being put off by your social media content, which can sometimes feel unnerving. As a seasoned professional, John-Paul feels that having a robust sense of self helps him navigate social media in general, and deems this an important part of the process.

We have provided this case example in addition to our later round-table discussion, to show how a private practitioner may use reflexivity in action, and how there are different ways, and different platforms, for all of us. Just like how as private practitioners we set up our business and market in a way that works uniquely for us (which reflects who we are), this extends to how we broaden our practice around social media.

Building private practice – collective support

Social media can be a great place to gain support in building your practice. Student projects such as Counselling Tutor on Facebook and #TraineeTalk (the student wing of #TherapistsConnect) on X/Twitter and Facebook are two options for trainees particularly in the latter stages of training, who are looking to meet others with an interest in going into private practice, as well as learning from the facilitators how one might navigate this. It creates opportunities for networking, development, and shared experiences at this crucial time, where preparing for working within this sector is so important. In addition, marketing-based resources such as the UK-based *Grow Your Private Practice* podcast by Jane Travis, and "Private Practice Pro" Instagram page by Kelley Stevens (based in the USA) provide valuable free tools and tips for private practitioners, outside of their chargeable products and services.

Hearing the voices of private practitioners

In the introduction, we argued that social media could be a force for good in promoting inclusivity. Isolation can be dangerous in many ways, and where the private practitioner is concerned, their position within our profession may throw up feelings of unbalanced power dynamics. Myira Khan describes power as:

> The ability to access and influence others, to act with autonomy and exercise control, to access resources, spaces and services.
>
> (Khan, 2023, p. 88)

Some of the issues around the systems that exist within the therapy professions (that we discussed in Chapter 4) are relevant when it comes to social media usage amongst private practitioners. If we imagine the life of a private practitioner, set in isolation and immersed purely in clinical practice, their general capacity to influence, and even be seen, may be limited. They may feel far away from regulatory bodies, or membership bodies, who, although are supposed to represent such practitioners, might instead feel like opposing forces. Feeling that your opinions about actual therapy practice (which you are mostly engaged in) are not being understood, heard, or acknowledged can be a difficult place for any human being. It's one of the principles we understand most as therapists working with clients! Kearney talked about the cultural frameworks that emerge from the social stratification that exists within our own systems. She explained how easy it is to take them as a given, especially if belonging to a relatively powerful group, who might be invested in not recognising the inequalities that exist (Kearney, 2018).

If we are to accept that there is an issue with unpaid work in this profession, which at times forces people into private practice, then we need to also accept the diverse needs of those many working practitioners. This includes the sector and its evolution as a whole, in addition to the unique, diverse cultural identities of these individual working professionals. Whilst some might question the role of private practitioners themselves in offering private services (and therefore arguably adding to an inequality problem in terms of who can access therapy), as authors we feel very strongly about championing therapists' own social needs. If therapists are having to work in the private sector because there is no other way to earn money, then their choice and freewill, within our own micro culture, is restricted. And so, we circle back around to power dynamics. Social media can be a vehicle for building solidarity between private practitioners, which is very powerful in terms of balancing out extremities of power. The same could be said of any networks, groups, communities, collectives – the aim being to empower private practitioners, as well as the future of this sector.

With all this in mind, it felt paramount that we included an informal discussion within this book, that heard the voices of private practitioners who are currently using social media:

Round-table discussion

This is an informal round-table discussion between private practitioners on the ethical considerations around the use of social media.

Participants for this round-table were recruited via a set of social media posts on Facebook, Instagram, and X/Twitter. The request was for therapists who are currently working as private practitioners and engaging relatively frequently on social media. Although the request was put out on just these three named platforms (due to the author's own restrictions, such as where they, themselves, currently hold accounts), an open invitation was made for participation from those using a broad array of social media platforms so as to bring a range of varied experiences. There was an agreement between participants where the purpose of the discussion was clearly laid out, alongside the intentions, and practicalities. In terms of how the conversation was conducted, it was felt that a peer-led reflective focus group approach would align with the philosophy of our book, particularly with our aim of giving a voice to working private practitioners. The option was given for the participants to remain anonymous if they so wished, so they would feel safe and comfortable contributing. However, all participants decided to be named.

Participants: Caz Binstead, Lukas Dressler, Paul Gilbert, Claudia Kempinska, Myira Khan, Emily McArthur, Sara Mathews

What are the ethical considerations of using social media for private practitioners (working within the field of counselling and psychotherapy), and how do participants make sense of their experience of engaging, with regards to their work and professional identity?

The discussion started with a general overview of which platforms the participants used, and their reasons for using them. Lukas Dressler told the group how isolation had formed a big part of this, and that social media could be used as a pathway to both virtual and in-person connection:

> The main reason why I became more active on Twitter, wasn't necessarily from a purely professional standpoint, but it was much more about the isolation that I felt, because I started my private practice just after the pandemic, so March/April 2021 … I had only just finished my training in Germany and then then moved back to Brighton. That was the initial motivation, to connect with therapists and psychologists in the UK (in Brighton and Hove), and to build my professional network. I felt lonely sitting in my apartment in front of the computer.
>
> (LD)

Emily McArthur concurred, saying that, for her, some social media platforms enabled her to build professional networks in her local area, helping not just with isolation, but also in growing and maintaining her private practice:

> Part of that for me was about meeting people so I could get referrals. Ultimately, I need business, and to work out who's in my local area, and who it is who is near me … to be able to say – do you want to get a coffee? I've built a local community of practitioners who I can now refer to and who refer to me.
>
> (EM)

It was agreed that the isolation in private practice was all-encompassing, with Paul Gilbert adding that he felt social media provided personal as well as professional links:

> Not only are people expressing things that are similar to you; a place where we're (ed. private practitioners) really almost suffering in isolation,

but lo and behold, they have other thoughts as well, and we connect on other things.

(PG)

As the conversation moved onto the types of social media platforms, it was clear that the group all used different types of platforms for different reasons. Sara Mathews spoke about her use of X/Twitter:

I certainly use Twitter as a way of feeling like I'm in the world, because I now only work in private practice ... I've picked up a lot of work via Twitter, certainly quite a few supervisees.

(SM)

Myira Khan spoke of LinkedIn having become a recent favourite of hers:

LinkedIn is all about conversation, and how I can generate conversation.

(MK)

With Claudia Kempinska explaining how being on Instagram helps them in their work, enabling them to keep abreast of what is happening within the communities of the main client group they work with:

To connect with the LGBTQ+ community for example, on Instagram – that's been super helpful, just to hear what's going on at ground level and what clients are experiencing within the community.

(CK)

Having reflected as a group on the multifaceted purposes of social media, we moved on to the importance of consideration and clarity around your intentions on each platform:

I'm thinking about the differences, and what type of connection we're seeking. So, Facebook for me, is not about connecting with other professionals, it's about connecting with potential clients. Twitter is purely about networking and meeting fellow professionals.

(EM)

There's an important topic around informed consent. If you have a huge presence on say, Instagram, and you provide psycho-educational material,

I'm sure clients may well contact you with whatever is on their mind. So, you then have to be really clear as to how you are using social media as part of your private practice. Asking, why am I on social media? How am I going to use it? And what are my boundaries and how do I communicate those to both professionals and clients.

(LD)

Picking up on these themes around intentions and boundaries, Caz Binstead, an avid social media user, with very large accounts on both Instagram and X/ Twitter, talks about her own process:

I always think – whatever I put on my social media – I have to feel 100% comfortable with. And that if a client came into the room and brought it up, I would be okay to talk about it.

(CB)

Digital policies were also discussed as an option. This can be not only be communicated in a client's first session, but also be visible on your website, to allow anyone to access it. The group felt in general that asking oneself these "what", "why", and "how" questions was a vital component of ethical practice on social media.

At this point, Caz summarises some of the themes around private practitioners' possible use of social media, focusing the conversation further into the types of ethical issues that might arise on social media:

Growing your practice and getting referrals; extending your own learning/ CPD; professional connection; developing your professional identity; combatting loneliness; campaigning; educating others; helping people out in the ether. So, taking all these into consideration, I wonder what ethical issues arise, particularly if we're using our different platforms for different things?

(CB)

The personal vs professional is the first theme picked up on:

How much do we disclose about our personal life? The boundaries and the cross-over between what's our professional identity, and what's our personal identity. And how much do we sometimes even use our personal identity to market our professional identity?

(LD)

His reply outlines the potential complexities for private practitioners in balancing, careful thought around personal self-disclosure, with the sometimes-purposeful entwining of our personal and professional identities.

On this, there was some disagreement in the group around whether it was necessary to have separate personal and professional accounts. Emily and Sara stated the following:

> The sheer value of being able to separate different accounts, and have something that is just a business account (and not personal). And for our personal accounts, being aware of any changes in the privacy settings on particular platforms. To be aware that if a private account is open, or they are not separate, the client might see something very personal.
>
> (EM)

> We're all kind of doing things slightly differently. I think for me, the key is that it is thought out, that whatever it is we're doing, we are thinking. And we are also mindful of the absent client, or the person "out there" (ed. prospective client), who may engage with us.
>
> (SM)

Reflecting on how useful it was to have a space to think with others about how to use social media in an ethical way, Paul expressed how intricately complex a simple share on social media could be:

> I could say something quite general, and yet it could really strike where the client is, and it could have a profound effect – in a good way, or a sensitive way.
>
> (PG)

Although the group agreed with this point, Sara also added the importance of the profession (and us), remembering that we are also human beings – that it's not always easy to get right, and mistakes may sometimes be made:

> It's a lot to hold. There are all the other ethical considerations in terms of our work, and this is just one dimension of ethical practice. I think we underestimate that massively, because there's an assumption that we've all got to be good at this. I think it's quite stressful for people – therapists can really stumble, and feel very, very anxious about how they are on a social media platform.
>
> (SM)

Claudia adds that the idea that we can never bring elements of our personal into the mix doesn't seem in line with how she views therapy practice, and reflects on returning to some of the basics laid down in our ethical codes:

> We're never a blank screen, are we? That's impossible. We need to be mindful of an intention that what we're sharing is of benefit, and, doing no harm.

And Myira made an interesting point about how we can use our ethical codes, and engage in ethical practice on social media, by imagining it as an extension of the client space:

> Viewing social media as a therapeutic space, and what I mean by that is, if, we're engaging with social media platforms, that actually becomes an extension of a therapeutic space, because we have to be there, following the same ethical guidelines and boundaries. I hadn't made this as explicit in my head before, but how I engage with social media and how I am on it, is how I am as a counsellor, because it's thinking about how I engage with this space in a way that is ethical.
>
> (MK)

In response to this, Paul demonstrated a way that you could think about your usage of social media through an ethical lens:

> What hat have we got on when we're doing something. I think a lot of the time I go to respond to something, and then I think, what's my intention, what am I trying to do? What am I hoping is going to happen, or am I just reacting?
>
> (PG)

We then moved onto confidentiality. It was observed that a Facebook group can often feel safe to share in (especially if the group settings are private), and yet, the ethical parameters around what is okay to share when it comes to our work can become blurred. It was felt that within such spaces there was a potential for confusion around the boundaries of the group – namely, that is not a supervision space. Confidentiality was something everyone agreed needed to be an absolute, in line with our ethical commitments as therapists.

Interestingly, though, breaches of confidentiality on the various social media platforms had been observed by the whole group. One fascinating discussion that was around "hypothetical" questions, that is, ones which do not technically break the confidentiality of a client but ask questions around things that could happen. There was some general scepticism about the use of "hypotheticals" by therapists. Paul stated:

You could argue that there are no hypotheticals!

(PG)

This is an interesting point when we consider what clients may see when they look at therapy discussions on social media. It could be very easy for a past or present client to trace something that is said as a "hypothetical" back to them.

Emily wondered if it served a role in the lessening of isolation in private practice:

For me, it loops back around to connection. Hypothetically, someone poses a question, but what they're actually doing, is connecting with their peers. They're finding a way to ask the things that are in their head, that they don't know where to put. They just want to have some people's responses to feed off, and the intention, ultimately, is connecting with the people around them.

(EM)

A conversation around this desire for connection between private practitioners followed, with questions around how that can be achieved safely, particularly in designated spaces, such as Facebook groups. It was pointed out that sometimes the shaming of therapists was prolific. The group felt that there was a responsibility for "Admins" of such groups, or "Community Leads", to be active – not just in drawing up group rules, but in ongoing engagement with their own social media policy. As an example of why this might be important, it was pointed out that even the definition of providing "support" for private practitioners could be disputed, with people holding differing views about what that even means. If an isolated private practitioner is seeking support of a particular kind (and is perhaps asking a question), but in response gets castigated for it by other group members, this would result in the exact opposite of connection.

We also pondered on the decisions (and accompanying process) that we might make around our personal life, where there is a potential cross-over with our work:

> I avoid being in LGBTQ+ social media groups so there's not a dual, triple, quadruple relationship, but I have to think about how that impacts on my personal life, because why should I remove myself from those arenas? Like for example, if I were to go to Pride, would some of my clients be there? Potentially, yes. But just like if I think there were to be a cross-over between the public and the private with any other aspect of a therapist's life, as long as it gets talked about how that's going to be managed, that's the important thing.
>
> (CK)

This fits with philosophy of our three-dimensional model, where it is acknowledged that ethical considerations, particularly in private practice, extend beyond just the client, and emphasise the importance of reflecting on the therapist's experience, as well as the wider social perspective. In smaller communities such as the LGBTQ+ community, there may be a greater impact on the therapist who feels the need to remove themselves from any place (including on social media) where they risk "bumping into" a client.

Another important point that was picked up on in the discussion was around the issue of lone working and safety. Private practitioners are particularly vulnerable given they are often working alone, and this is something that needs thought and pre-emptive action when using social media:

> The other thing is around self-disclosure, and how we keep ourselves safe. Thinking about private practice, often we work in isolated settings, so we might be working in a building at night by ourselves. There's elements of safety that are particular to our field of practice, and when we're thinking about self-disclosure, there's lots of different elements of safety that start to come into that. That has a real relevance to us as a community.
>
> (EM)

It is well-known on ground level that the safety of some private practitioners has, at times, been compromised. This is a very real, and serious thing. Private practitioners need to be aware that whatever they put publicly on their social media sites can be seen by anyone. Being vigilant and cognisant that even our business details might be used for opportunistic criminal behaviour such as inappropriate phone-calls feels important. In addition, therapists who are very active on social media may also wish to be mindful of how much they know about the people who interact with them (and with whom they may interact back with). Putting in more robust boundaries when needed, and, if something doesn't feel right, speaking to someone you trust, is recommended. The therapy profession in general (the bodies and regulators) surely has much more work to do in helping to protect the safety of private practitioners, and in engaging in an active approach, which directly supports those affected.

The discussion ended with some thoughts around how social media, and its use by private practitioners may evolve:

> I think the platforms and the way they get used may change. But I think particularly in private practice, it forms such a way to connect – the sharing of ideas, networking, the finding out about CPD events, attracting clients: it's a way of running a business now, it's part of our job. Some people use it to varying degrees, but it's definitely not going anywhere. Ethically speaking, what is the burden of responsibility on us to keep up with technology and understand it? How can we use a social media platform, if we don't understand its privacy. How much is it our responsibility to learn about VR (virtual reality) and AI (artificial intelligence)? Is it our responsibility to practice these technologies because clients may be using them – even if we opt out of social media? I don't think that we can ignore it as being part of our world
>
> (EM)

> Social media will always be there, and we'll always be utilising it as private practitioners, but I wonder how we might engage in those spaces. I'm thinking about VR. Will we be in a place where we'll be sat in our rooms but with a headset, and then physically moving around and having a coffee with one another? We'll end up having a virtual space, with our avatars!
>
> (MK)

Paul agreed with Myira's vision:

> As much as I'm against AI for therapy, I think that's something I could get onboard with … when you see the whole person!! It's something else to work with. I don't know where it will go, but we need to change and evolve with it.
>
> (PG)

In conclusion, taking into consideration the entire discussion, the *convergent themes were as follows*:

- That social media helped to alleviate loneliness and isolation.
- That relationships between private practitioners could be forged online, bringing support and enhancing community.
- That although private practitioner's using social media could be supportive, it could also, at times, work the other way.
- That social media connected us with other private partitioners, as well as potential clients, and so also played a part in growing business.
- That some kind of informed consent or digital policy was needed. It was generally agreed by all, that thinking through your engagement with social media carefully, including the different uses for different platforms, was crucial.
- That maintaining confidentiality, ought to be a number one priority for private practitioners.
- That although Facebook counselling groups can help in reducing isolation, they can also be problematic, and that an acknowledgement of the limitations of Facebook groups was needed.
- That "containment" (being aware of how we contain our own emotion and processes, including reactions), and an awareness of our own transferential responses, such as projection, played an important role in how a private practitioner, on some of the more "conversation-based" platforms (such as X/Twitter), could engage in an ethical way.
- That social media will always be here.

Some of the divergent points were:

- The group's choice of social media platforms, and how/why they used them.
- The pragmatics around social media, with some members posting the same things across their various social media platforms; some pre-scheduling their posts; and some engaging only in a "live" way.
- Whether it was beneficial or not, to separate personal and professional accounts.
- That a digital policy was the only way to manage social media use, and ought to be a compulsory part of a private practitioner's paperwork (three members of the group at the time, had such a policy in place).

- Opinions about whether disinhibition (and private practitioner's experience of) is necessarily always relevant to, and more prevalent, online.
- The extent to which the private practitioner had an ongoing duty to be continually vigilant in their social media use, in order to be an ethical practitioner, and uphold professional standards.

This was a useful discussion which pulled together some of the considerations around ethical use of social media by private practitioners. It's worth noting that this is an evolving arena for therapists, and there is much more research and work to be done in the area. Although the information that has been collated is, we hope, useful to long-term professional discussions around this topic, on a personal level, the group felt that just having the space to talk, think through, and debate with others formed part of helping them reflect. It therefore in itself contributed to the development of their own ongoing ethical decision-making. We'll end with this quote by Myira, which sums up some of the author's thoughts around the importance of social media for private practitioners:

> This is about belonging. A transition into private practice, re-shapes and re-structures us in our relationship with the profession. And so I think social media takes on a really significant role for us that means that we might ourselves belong in the profession. To feel that we belong, as part of this community.
>
> (MK)

TAKE-AWAY MESSAGES: Social media has opened up a whole new world for private practitioners, which is ever expanding. But this doesn't come without its ethical dilemmas. See if you can stick to using hypothetical scenarios in conversations online for practical issues around private practice only, instead of actual client work. And be ever reflective of how and why you use social media. Remember, your modality may inform how you interact, especially around considerations such as self-disclosure, so being aware of your own boundaries and intentions is crucial.

References

Blundell, P., Binstead, C. (2023). *Three years of #TherapistsConnect. The #TherapistsConnect Podcast.* www.therapists-connect.com/podcast/episode/7864a d9d/three-years-of-therapistsconnect

Kearney, A. (2018). *Counselling, class and politics: Undeclared influences in therapy* (Revised). PCCS Books.

Khan, M. (2023). *Working within diversity: A reflective guide to anti-oppressive practice in counselling and therapy.* Jessica Kingsley.

White, E., Hanley, T. (2023). Current ethical dilemmas experienced by therapists who use social media: A systematic review. *Counselling and Psychotherapy Research,* 24(2), 396–418. https://doi.org/10.1002/capr.12678

Epilogue

Caz Binstead and Nicholas Sarantakis

At the end of our book, we leave you with this quote from Linda Finlay, which, for us, sums up relational ethics:

> Virtually every ethical issue and dilemma we encounter can be answered with the phrase, 'it depends'. … [R]elational ethics drive us towards collaborative, responsive, respectful, compassionate and authentic relationships as opposed to exploitative, instrumental or habitual ones.
>
> (Finlay, 2019, pp. 3–4)

Ethical practice is a creative process; a flowing well that springs from the core values we hold dear to therapy practice. Values such as integrity, empathy, and humility towards our clients will go far in guiding us through the complexities of our work, as well as recognising and tackling the more nuanced ethical dilemmas that a private practitioner, specifically, may face. We hope we have shown that ethical practice is often about being unafraid to expose and engage with some of the more taboo subjects. In fact, it may feel somewhat ironic that being ethical often comes from working directly with realistic truths that arise from this messy – and not straight-forward – human world. A respect for all humankind, however, will allow us to afford similar core principles and values to ourselves, as private practitioners, as well as to wider societal issues, whilst we navigate the sometimes very tricky job of setting up and maintaining our private practices. We hope you find the three-dimensional model a useful vehicle for putting ethical codes and frameworks into practice, and for developing the essential reflexivity skills that we need to effectively engage with ethics in action.

DOI: 10.4324/9781003435624-12

Wishing you the all the best in developing your 21st-century, unique, ethical private practices.

Caz and Nicholas

Reference

Finlay, L. (2019). *Practical ethics in counselling and psychotherapy: A relational approach* (pp. 3–4). Sage.

Chapter biographies

Textbook authors

Caz Binstead is an experienced private practitioner, supervisor, and facilitator/visiting lecturer. Specialising in the growth and maintenance of ethical and thriving practice, she was instrumental in the creation of the Private practice toolkit at the British Association for Counselling and Psychotherapy (BACP) and acted as divisional lead on the project. Caz is co-lead of the community platform #TherapistsConnect, and was creative director on their two-day conference, "Private practice 2021: surviving and thriving in uncertain times". Through her extensive work in this area, Caz has helped hundreds of therapists with their private practices.

Nicholas Sarantakis is a practising counselling psychologist and couple, family, and group therapist in London and Milton Keynes. He is the author of several academic and professional articles in psychology and psychotherapy. He has taught at five UK universities as Senior Lecturer and Director of Studies. www.nicholassarantakis.com

Contributors

Susan Dale is BACP's Ethics Lead and is Project Lead for the Ethical Framework review. She has also worked on the previous two reviews of the Framework and is passionate about ethics. Alongside her work for BACP she is a BACP accredited counsellor with a small private practice. She lives and works in the Scottish Highlands. Following her training as a counsellor in the early 1990s she undertook an MSc in Counselling and then went on to study narrative therapy and life story research, culminating in a Doctorate in Education at Bristol University in 2009.

John-Paul Davies is a therapist running a full-time practice from Cobham, Surrey, UK, having previously worked as a solicitor in the City of London. He has published a self-help book, *Finding a Balanced Connection*, and written about a range of wellbeing and psychological topics for various media.

Lukas Dressler (he/him) is committed to fostering wellbeing for children, adolescents, and adults in a compassionate space. He is an HCPC registered Counselling Psychologist, Member of WPATH, and specialises in working with ADHD and gender identity as well as depression and anxiety.

Paul Gilbert is an integrative psychotherapist, clinical supervisor and trainer, who studied at The Sherwood Institute. Paul works within the NHS and private practice. He has set up and managed services for national mental health charities and worked in both acute, PICU, and forensic settings. He has a great interest in the developmental unconscious processes that influence our relationships due to our past experience. www.pauljgilbertcounsellingandpsychotherapy.com/

Claudia Kempinska is a psychodynamic psychotherapist and EMDR practitioner. Claudia has worked in private practice for nine years, specialising in trauma and gender identity.

Myira Khan is an accredited counsellor, supervisor, trainer, Founder of the Muslim Counsellor and Psychotherapist Network (MCAPN) and author of *Working Within Diversity – A Reflective Guide to Anti-Oppressive Practice in Counselling and Therapy* (published July 2023).

Emily McArthur is a senior accredited counsellor and supervisor working in Leamington Spa, Warwickshire. She has been in private practice for the past eight years, and works with adults and young people aged 18+.

Sara Mathews is an experienced therapist and supervisor now in private practice. Sara spent many years heading up bereavement services in hospices. She is a qualified teacher, taught in the university sector, managed an alcohol rehabilitation centre, and delivered training for creative clinical supervision. Sara also has a degree in drama and bakes a very good sourdough! https://saramathewscounselling.co.uk/

Index

accessibility 99–100; money issues 100–101; online therapy 73–74, 76, 99
accreditations: contracts 61; marketing 49–51
administration *see* practice management
advertising *see* marketing
agreements *see* contracts
alcohol dependency 63
American Psychological Association (APA) 48
artificial intelligence (AI) 35, 143
assessments *see* initial sessions/ assessments
audio calls 73–74

Black Lives Matter 95
boundaries *see* practice boundaries
British Association for Counselling and Psychotherapy (BACP): client focus 3; clinical wills 31; *Code of Ethics and Practice for Counsellors* 40; complaints 34–35, 68–69, 113; contract template 62; endings 108, 113; Ethical Framework for the Counselling Professionals 35, 36, 41, 51, 69, 124; Ethics Service 34; marketing 40, 41, 48; membership demographics 9; Professional Conduct 34–35; Professional Standards 34; registration 33; resources 9–10, 17, 27, 33, 62; testimonials 48; Workforce Mapping Survey 1, 9

British Psychological Society (BPS) 34
burn-out 114; money issues 100–101, 104; supervision 120–123
business cards 45–46

cancellations: contracts 62; practice boundaries 64, 67–68
client notes 33–34; initial session paperwork 27–29
climate change 95–96
clinical associates 16
clinical executors 31–32
clinical wills 30–32
codes of ethics 2, 23; clinical wills 30; contracts 68; couple's, family, and group therapy 80–81, 85; marketing 40, 48–51; record keeping 33; social media 140; testimonials 48
complaints: BACP 34–35, 68–69, 113; independent bodies 50; practice boundaries 68–70; premature endings 113; verbal contracts 55
concessionary slots 100–101
confidence: group therapy 90; public, in therapists 60; responding to potential clients 61; risk assessment 29; starting in private practice 17, 18
confidentiality: AI industry 35; breaches 30–31, 34, 62, 141; client notes 34; clinical wills 31; contract 30, 57, 62; family therapy 84; group therapy 90–91; social media 140–141, 144; supervision notes 33; testimonials 48

T - #0022 - 061124 - C0 - 210/148/10 - PB - 9781032564593 - Matt Lamination